The Gospel Tradition

The Gospel Tradition

Essays by HARALD RIESENFELD

Foreword by W. D. DAVIES

FORTRESS PRESS Philadelphia

The translation of eight chapters of this book, from Swedish and French, was made by E. Margaret Rowley; the translation of one chapter, from German, was made by Robert A. Kraft.

Library of Congress Catalog Card Number 74–101429

2313H69   Printed in U.S.A.   1-231

Contents

Foreword

Geographically, Scandinavian countries can be thought of as lying on the northern outposts of Europe, slightly outside the main body of the Continent. But theologically it is impossible to think of them as thus apart. They have not only welcomed and responded creatively to the stimuli of international scholarship, but have also, in turn, confronted the whole theological world with the challenge of their own peculiar insights. In no sphere is this more true than in that of biblical studies. It is true of all the Scandinavian countries and, not least, of Sweden. The impact of Swedish scholarship on the interpretation of the Old and New Testament in our time, both through the publication of learned and sometimes epoch-making books, as well as through the nurture of significant theological teachers who have left their native shores, has been profound and widespread.

To this Scandinavian and particularly Swedish tradition of both reacting and acting scholarship belongs Professor Harald Riesenfeld. On the one hand, he reveals a receptive openness to all the scholarly winds that blow from outside his own land; on the other, he reveals the characteristics of the Scandinavian scholar—a sensitivity to the total background of the biblical documents in the Near East and to living oral tradition as their matrix, a finesse in detecting echoes and reechoes of motifs in the tradition that emerge in one form, are in time submerged only to re-emerge in other related forms, and an awareness of the religious dimensions of the documents concerned.

It is, therefore, a great privilege for me to be allowed to write this brief foreword. Professor Riesenfeld's name needs

Foreword

no introduction to American readers, but it was necessary that some of his work, often scattered in inaccessible or untranslated periodicals and pamphlets, should be gathered in an easily available volume, so that the peculiar 'flavor' and 'style' of Dr. Riesenfeld's writing might be even more widely known. We congratulate the Fortress Press on making such a volume possible.

W. D. DAVIES

Duke University
Durham, North Carolina
November 1969

Acknowledgments

I am grateful to the following for permission to reprint the substance of articles which have previously appeared:

Akademie-Verlag, Berlin, for chapter 1 ("The Gospel Tradition and Its Beginnings" in *Studia Evangelica*, Texte und Untersuchungen zur Geschichte der altchristlichen Literatur, Band 73, 1959); and for chapter 8 ("Das Bildwort vom Weizenkorn bei Paulus [zu 1 Cor. 15]" in *Studien zum Neuen Testament und zur Patristik*, Erich Klostermann zum 90. Geburtstag dargebracht, Texte und Untersuchungen zur Geschichte der altchristlichen Literatur, Band 77, 1961);

Cambridge University Press, Cambridge and New York, for chapter 2 ("The Mythological Background of New Testament Christology" in *The Background of the New Testament and Its Eschatology*, Studies in Honor of C. H. Dodd, edited by W. D. Davies and D. Daube, 1956);

Desclée de Brouwer, Bruges, for chapter 4 ("Le Caractère Messianique de la Tentation au Désert" in *La Venue du Messie*—Messianisme et Eschatologie, Recherches Bibliques VI); and for chapter 9 ("Le Langage Parabolique dans les Épitres de Saint Paul" in *Littérature et Théologie Pauliniennes, Recherches Bibliques* V);

Svensk Exegetisk Årsbok for chapter 3 ("Till Markusevangeliets komposition" in XVIII–XIX, 1953–54); chapter 5 ("Perikopen *de adultera* i den fornkyrkliga traditionen" in XVII, 1952); and for chapter 7 ("Liknelserna i den synoptiska och i den johanneiska traditionen" in XXV, 1960);

Religion och bibel for chapter 6 ("Sabbat och Herrens

Acknowledgments

dag i judendomen, Jesu förkunnelse och urkristendomen" in Nathan Söderblom-Sällskapets årsbok, XVIII, 1959).

I am also grateful to Statens Humanistiska Forskningsråd of the Royal Swedish Government for its generous assistance in making the translation of these articles possible. I am, of course, deeply appreciative of the translations prepared by Miss Margaret Rowley of Näsby Park, Sweden, and Professor Robert A. Kraft of the University of Pennsylvania, Philadelphia. Finally, it is a pleasure to express my gratitude to my friend, W. D. Davies of Duke University, for the encouragement and wise judgment he has shown throughout the development of this collection.

H. R.

Uppsala, Sweden
Summer 1969

I. The Gospel Tradition
   and Its Beginnings

The inexhaustible significance of the Gospels lies pre-
eminently in the fact that they are our principal source for
any account of the life of Jesus. The sparse biographical
data in the rest of the New Testament writings and in the
other early Christian and non-Christian literature, though
they may have a certain interest of their own, contribute
nothing to our conception of the figure of Christ. The question is often raised whether there is not something unfitting
in the fact that our account of the life of Christ should
have come down to us not in a single Gospel, but in four,
and, what is more, in accounts which differ in some of their
details. Should we not have been better served by a single
Gospel? To such questions we must reply emphatically
"No!" Had this been the case, we should have been seriously
perplexed whether we were not in the presence of a literary
fiction or, in any case, of a very subjective interpretation
of the figure the Gospels depict. It is by reason of the fact
that we have several, to be precise four, accounts, that we
have been granted a more sharply defined and a more
realistic presentation of the person of Jesus, just as in a
stereoscope we obtain a far superior three-dimensional impression from pictures which, when examined side by side
without the lens, differ among themselves. These differences
between the Gospels naturally create for the student a
never-ending problem; but for our assurance of the historic-
ity of Jesus and for our general knowledge of who and
what he was, the fact that we have a plurality of four
Gospels is a fundamental advantage.

Now what precisely is a Gospel? In the history of religion and of literature alike a Gospel is something wholly unique. It is true that there are distant parallels in the biographies of philosophers or rulers in the Greek literature of the Hellenistic age. This is more particularly so in the case of St. Luke's Gospel, the only one of the four which has been in any degree molded by literary considerations. On the other hand, there exist certain parallels on Palestinian soil, notably in the prophetic books of the Old Testament. Here we have parallels, in matters of outward form, to the preaching of Jesus and to his appearances before his hearers as these are portrayed in the Gospels. But none of these parallels takes us beyond individual items. To the Gospels as a whole there is no known parallel or analogy. The same negative verdict is given by the much-discussed and much-debated manuscripts from the Dead Sea. It is true that in these new texts we have data which assist our understanding of primitive Christianity, its mode of thought and its method of organization, its writings and its vocabulary, for we owe them to a religious movement in Judaism roughly contemporary with Jesus of which we have been hitherto almost wholly unaware. There is also much in the New Testament whose origin was previously sought in distant countries, such as the Johannine symbolism of light and darkness or the ministerial offices in the early Christian communities, which has now been proved to be the native product of Palestine. We also have in the writings of the so-called Sect countless instructive parallels to the very free way in which primitive Christianity often used and interpreted its quotations from the Old Testament. But how gratified we should have been to have discovered among these texts and fragments a Gospel concerned with the leading figure in this Jewish movement, the so-called Teacher of Righteousness. Yet of such a Gospel we have found no trace. And it is certain that we shall find none.

Now where did our Gospels come from? Obviously it is no sufficient answer to say that they came from their evangelists' pens. It is true that the Gospels in their several forms are the products of writers and theologians who were consciously creative. And to this extent we can reckon either with individual authors or with circles or schools from which one or more of the Gospels came. In the former class we must certainly put Luke and probably also Mark, both of them Gospels which reflect certain individual characteristics either of their actual authors or of the early tradition from which they came; in the other class perhaps the Gospels of Matthew and John which issued from the formative influence of a school. But what each of the four evangelists has done is to create this or that Gospel, with its characteristic marks, with its individual style, its structure, its theology, and its peculiar features in its picture of Jesus. Nevertheless, it is no chance that the titles given to the Gospels in the early church were: "The Gospel According to Matthew," "The Gospel According to Mark," and so on. The evangelists took over their material from the tradition as it lay before them. And though it may be possible to establish points of interdependence in the existing Gospels, none of the four is the religious or literary prototype of the Gospel proper; this must be sought in their prehistory which is not directly accessible to us. It is important to recognize, as is clear from a study of the extant Gospels, that the tradition which lay before our evangelists already had the characteristic *traits* of the class of literature which we describe as Gospels, and that even if it had not yet reached full definition, it could nonetheless be already identified as such.

We shall not endeavor to deal here with the origin of the several Gospels in their present form, each with its own

3

characteristics. To do so would be to enter upon four far-reaching and separate fields of study. What we shall attempt to do is, with the aid of the material embodied in our four Gospels, to make clear the prehistory and, as far as we can, the very beginnings of the tradition which finds its written embodiment in the Gospels as they have come down to us. How then did the tradition arise, the tradition of the words and deeds of Jesus? Where shall we find its "situation in life" [*Sitz im Leben*]?

Nearly forty years ago an important hypothesis was propounded to answer this question. Though at the time it opened up new and fruitful paths of study, and in many respects was of abiding importance, yet in its one-sidedness it became one of those scientific dogmas or myths which have their day and then must gradually be set aside if they are not to impede the further development of investigation. I am here referring, of course, to the solution put forward by the so-called form criticism. The names of the distinguished scholars associated with this school are well-known to all professional students of the Gospels. What concerns us here is the subject more than personalities.[1] The permanent achievement of form-critical investigation is the formal analysis of the individual elements in the Gospel material, of the parables and other words of Jesus, of the accounts of the deeds of Jesus, or of happenings in the life of Jesus. These elements were assembled from the tradition which was originally oral, but gradually, as time went on, also written down, and then transmitted, as individual fragments or in small groups, until they found their final

---

[1]See, e.g., Martin Dibelius, *From Tradition to Gospel*, trans. from rev. 2nd ed. Bertram L. Woolf (New York: Charles Scribner's Sons, 1935); K. L. Schmidt, *Der Rahmen der Geschichte Jesu* (Berlin: 1919); Rudolf Bultmann, *The History of the Synoptic Tradition*, trans. John Marsh (New York: Harper & Row, 1963), p. 63; E. Fascher, *Die formgeschichtliche Methode* (1924); P. Benoit, "Reflexions sur la 'formgeschichtliche Methode,'" *Rev. Bibl.* 53 (1946): 481–542.

embodiment in the compilations known to us as our Gospels. From these studies we now know, for instance, that a parable or an account of a miracle took shape in accordance with definite stylistic laws which can be seen at work in transformations of all items of the same kind. And from our knowledge of these laws we can better appreciate and judge the peculiarities of the several evangelists. One fact of the first importance which we have learned is that these elements of tradition have been subjected to certain influences through the church life of the particular place or milieu where they were handed down or received their final written form. Thus by studying details of expression in the pericope on Martha and Mary in Luke 10, it is possible to recognize questions which arose about the position of women in the communities and on the importance of *diakonia.*

But often the exponents of form criticism went further than this. They held that their method enabled them to explain the very beginnings of the Gospel tradition. To this question, "What was the situation in life of the earliest Gospel tradition?" their answer was "preaching" or "catechetical instruction" or "controversy." This was because the first missionaries of the new movement that suddenly arose from belief in the resurrection were at once forced to base their preaching on the words of Jesus or on accounts of events in the life of the great Master of Nazareth. This solution presupposes an extraordinary creative capacity in the first Christian generations. A considerable part of the material which is contained in the Gospel was freely invented and then given definite shape. We may take an instance of the way in which the origin of the miracle stories was conceived. When Christianity made its way outside Palestine, into the wide area of the Mediterranean world with its Hellenistic culture, the Christian missionaries found themselves competing with wandering preachers of salvation and miracle workers of a Greco-Oriental type. They therefore felt it incumbent on them to present the greatness and importance of the Christ whom they proclaimed by the same means as those which their competing miracle men employed. To this end they invented stories of miraculous acts done by Jesus and thus conveyed to their hearers a striking impression of the power of their savior.

I cannot enter here into a detailed critique of these theories. The very existence of such an anonymous creative generation in primitive Christianity presupposes, in view of what we know from the New Testament about the apostles and the other members of the early Christian community, a truly miraculous and incredible factor in the history of the Gospel tradition. And the hypothesis that the miracle narratives arose on Hellenistic soil can be directly refuted. If we analyze the motives which form the content of the miracle narratives—and we must interpret the miracles as actions with a symbolic purpose which have their clear counterparts in the analogous symbolic acts of the Old Testament prophets—we find that the symbolism of all the miracles which occur and are described in the Gospels rests on a genuine Old Testament and Jewish basis. It certainly did not arise somewhere in the Hellenistic world. It is in just such points that the improved methods of observation of the last few years have succeeded in correcting the false conclusions of earlier students. Indeed, the analysis of the language of symbolism as we find it in the New Testament offers us far more reliable guidance in determining the modes of thought of the primitive tradition.

Another point to be noted is that modern judgments essentially inapplicable to the material under consideration are introduced into these analyses. Scholars have set out from a conception of Jesus which has been constructed a priori and have then asked what portions of the Gospel material accord with this conception. They have more or less unconsciously used as the measure of their inquiry what Jesus can or cannot have done, without taking account of the fact that from the very first the tradition understood the deeds no less than the words of Jesus as something wholly unique which can be understood only in an eschatological setting. But an imperative requirement in the matter of method is that the nature of the investigation, and the criteria by which the material is judged, should be appropriate to the subject of inquiry. And this is something that we can now see more clearly than was possible a few decades ago.[2]

But—to come at last to the main point—was mission preaching in the earliest years of Christianity one of the principal sources from which the Gospel tradition derived? We must ask the scholars who have reached this conclusion whether they have not allowed themselves to be influenced unawares by picturing in their minds a preacher of our own times. They have in view a conscientious pastor who, unrestrained by any prescribed lectionary, searches out a suitable text for his Sunday sermon. So, they suppose, it must have happened nineteen hundred years ago—except that on many occasions the text could not be found ready-made at all, but had first to be invented. But this picture, surely, is scarcely credible.

Nor, indeed, need we rest content with such general considerations. Scientific study of the material puts in our hands the means of demonstrable proof based on empirical facts. It is now many years since C. H. Dodd showed that

[2]Cf., e.g., Floyd V. Filson, *The New Testament Against Its Environment* (London SCM Press, 1950), pp. 43–50.

we can, as it were, distill from the speeches of the apostles in the first chapters of Acts characteristic elements of the earliest Christian preaching.[3] The content and final challenge of this preaching, whose object was to win its hearers to faith in Jesus Christ and which is hence commonly known as mission preaching, constitutes the so-called *kerygma*, a compressed summary of the saving work of Christ. Its content was as follows: " 'Jesus of Nazareth, a man attested to you by God with mighty works and wonders and signs which God did through him in your midst, as you yourselves know—this Jesus, delivered up according to the definite plan and foreknowledge of God, you crucified and killed by the hands of lawless men. But God raised him up, having loosed the pangs of death, because it was not possible for him to be held by it. . . . This Jesus God raised up, and of that we all are witnesses. Being therefore exalted at the right hand of God, and having received from the Father the promise of the Holy Spirit, he has poured out this which you see and hear. . . . Let all the house of Israel therefore know assuredly that God has made him both Lord and Christ, this Jesus whom you crucified.' Now when they heard this they were cut to the heart" (Acts 2:22–24, 32–33, 36–37). We have here typical elements in the primitive Christian preaching: a summary of the redemptive act, developed in close relationship to the religious situation of the hearers, and the whole culminating in a missionary reference, and insistence on the imperative need for conversion and faith. As far as the mission preaching to the Jews is concerned, the point of contact was, on the one hand, demonstration from Old Testament citations that Jesus is in very truth the promised Messiah who now exercises his dominion as the risen One,

[3]C. H. Dodd, *The Apostolic Preaching and Its Developments* (London: Hodder & Stoughton, 1936).

and, on the other, the threat of the final judgment, which all Jews awaited with fear, as directly imminent and the proclamation of salvation in this judgment through faith in the Messiah Jesus. Such was the mission preaching as it was directed to Jews. But in the same Book of Acts we have also pointers, at any rate, to the preaching to the Gentiles, as it was set forth, among others, by Paul, the great Gentile missionary. It is probable that Paul's so-called Areopagus speech at Athens represents, to some extent, an abbreviated and schematized, yet nonetheless typical, example of such a sermon to the Gentiles in Pauline modes of thought.[4] And here again we find direct contact made with the religious presuppositions of the hearers, though in this case they were different: "For as I passed along and observed the objects of your worship, I found also an altar with this inscription, 'To an unknown God.' What therefore you worship as unknown, this I proclaim to you. The God who made the world and everything in it, being Lord of heaven and earth, does not live in shrines made by man" (Acts 17:23–24). And then at the end, with the demand for conversion, we have a reference to precisely the preaching of Jesus Christ: "But now he commands all men everywhere to repent, because he has fixed a day on which he will judge the world in righteousness by a man whom he has appointed, and of this he has given assurance to all men by raising him from the dead" (17:30–31). Msgr. Lucien Cerfaux has accurately observed how Paul in his earlier letters, where he sets out from the Jewish situation, makes the fear of the approaching judgment the principal point of contact with his hearers in his mission preaching, whereas in his later letters he has chiefly in the foreground the fear of death, which was the question of existential

---

[4]See Bertil Gärtner, *The Areopagus Speech and Natural Revelation* (Copenhagen: Einar Munksgaard Forlag, 1955).

import in the Hellenistic world that knew little of the threat of judgment.[5]

Thus, with the help of Acts and of certain echoes in the New Testament Epistles, we can construct notions of the early Christian missionary preaching to Jews and Gentiles alike. And, as we have already said, we have fragments of kerygmatic formulas about the saving work of Christ. But of anything which recalls the materials from which our Gospels were constructed we have (alas!) not the least trace. It is true that claims have sometimes been made to have recovered them. For instance, there is a passage about Jesus put into the mouth of Peter in Acts 10 where we read: "You know the word which he sent to Israel, preaching good news of peace by Jesus Christ (he is Lord of all), the word which was proclaimed throughout all Judea, beginning from Galilee after the baptism which John preached: how God anointed Jesus of Nazareth with the Holy Spirit and with power; how he went about doing good and healing all that were oppressed by the devil, for God was with him. And we are witnesses to all that he did both in the country of the Jews and in Jerusalem. They put him to death by hanging him on a tree" (Acts 10:36–39). May not this summary of the life and death of Jesus be conceived as an epitome, so to speak, of the Gospel tradition? And could not the latter have been expanded from such rudiments into its later fullness? Along these lines the course of development is often still conceived. But is not such a solution another hypothetical dogma or myth? Facts are wholly wanting to support such a process of expansion, and there is certainly nothing in our Gospels, especially if we compare the three Synoptics with

[5]L. Cerfaux, *Le Christ dans la théologie de Saint Paul* (1951), pp. 45, 90 ff., 121 f., 125. An English translation of this book, *Christ in the Theology of St. Paul*, appeared in 1959 (trans. Geoffrey Webb and Adrian Walker, New York: Herder & Herder).

the Fourth Gospel, which gives the slightest basis for such a hypothesis. Here we must refrain from adducing further considerations and summarize our conclusion: mission preaching was not the *Sitz im Leben* of the Gospel tradition.

Side by side with mission preaching the announcement of the gospel went on within the Christian communities. On the one hand, there was the instruction of catechumens, on the other, edification of the community's members. This preaching in the framework of the communities took place not so much through appeal to the emotions as by instruction in matters of fact and in the Christian way of living. This teaching would have included both christological and other theological matters as well as ethical admonitions, this last in the form of the so-called parenesis. In this connection, we may recall, for instance, the catalogues of virtues and vices and also the "household instructions" [*Haustafeln*]. Nor are we here wholly dependent on speculation. From certain of the New Testament Epistles—especially the non-Pauline ones—we can see to some extent what the subject matter of such preaching was. For there can be no doubt that these Epistles were composed and dispatched to be read in the communities as formal utterances, that is, as sermons. And while it is certain that few unwritten sermons, in the matter either of content or form, could be compared with the letters of Paul, yet in respect of the species and kind of utterance, we can assuredly here build on analogies.

We have now to ask: Can we find in this preaching within the framework of the communities the primitive Gospel tradition? Here, too, scholars have sought to draw positive conclusions. Thus in 1 Corinthians 7:10 f., Paul expressly appeals to Jesus' teaching on marriage: "To the married I give charge, not I but the Lord, that the wife should not separate from her husband (but if she does, let her remain single or else be reconciled to her husband)—and that the husband should not divorce his wife." Doubtless the apostle is appealing here to the words of Jesus on marriage transmitted, e.g., in Mark 10. The situation is still clearer in the Epistle of James, where at almost every step we meet with allusions to parenetic sayings of Jesus. Have we not a proof here that in any case the sayings of Jesus with an ethical import were transmitted, if indeed they were not created, in connection with the early Christian parenesis? Yet this is another conclusion which I find it hard to accept for the following reasons, mainly based on considerations issuing from recent studies carried out in Uppsala.[6]

For if we suppose the existence of such an interrelation between early Christian community preaching and Gospel tradition, then it remains inexplicable that, while in the christological and parenetic parts of the New Testament Epistles we have countless allusions to the sayings of Jesus (though not to the narrative material of the Gospels), we have no express citations of his words. There can be only one explanation of this strange fact, namely, that the primitive Christian letter writers, and among them Paul, took express pains to avoid citing the sayings of Jesus in the context of their original utterance. Their method, that is, was directly the opposite of that of preachers of our own day. The sayings of Jesus, and hence the tradition about Jesus, were presumed to be already known, but this tradition was not cited in its verbal form.

Two examples will illustrate this point. Let us compare James 2:5: "Listen, my beloved brethren. Has not God chosen those who are poor in the world to be rich in faith and heirs of the kingdom . . . ?" with Matthew 5:3, 5:

---

[6]Birger Gerhardsson, *Memory and Manuscript* (2nd ed.; Lund, Sweden: C.W.K. Gleerup, 1964).

"Blessed are the poor in spirit, for theirs is the kingdom of heaven. . . . Blessed are the meek, for they shall inherit the earth." And again the saying in James 1:25: "But he who looks into the perfect law, the law of liberty, and perseveres, being no hearer that forgets but a doer that acts, he shall be blessed in his doing," has its counterpart in John 13:17: "If you know these things, blessed are you if you do them." Of the eight Matthean beatitudes, four are to be found in James and in the same order, a fact, by the way, which cannot be accidental. In any case the author of this Epistle presupposes parts of the Sermon on the Mount as clearly well-known to his readers. Indeed, we can establish that the verbal form of the sayings of Jesus which James presupposes is that of Matthew and not of Luke.

From the analysis of Paul's Epistles there is much that might be adduced on this subject, though here we must confine ourselves to a few brief remarks. It is clear that Paul was acquainted with the tradition of the sayings of Jesus, and at many points in his Epistles makes express allusion to sayings of his. This means in turn that Paul could presuppose these sayings as known to his readers. The words in Romans 12:14: "Bless those who persecute you; bless and do not curse them," are simply a paraphrase of the saying of Jesus: "Love your enemies and pray for those who persecute you" (Matt. 5:44). Hence scholars have concluded—and certainly correctly—that such a section as Romans 14:13 ff. records parenetic words of Jesus and that the Epistles to the Thessalonians have their basis in apocalyptic teaching in the synoptic tradition.[7]

---

[7]See, e.g., W. D. Davies, *Paul and Rabbinic Judaism* (2nd ed. 1956; London: SPCK, 1948), pp. 136 ff.; E. Earle Ellis, *Paul's Use of the Old Testament* (Grand Rapids: Eerdman's, 1957), pp. 86–92; George R. Beasley-Murray, *Jesus and the Future* (New York: St. Martin's Press, 1954), pp. 232–34—cf. Edward G. Selwyn, *The First Epistle of St. Peter* (London: Macmillan, 1946), pp. 23 f., 158 f., 268 ff., 376 ff., 442–49.

Once we have perceived this, very wide vistas open up. It is one of the characteristic features of the New Testament that the messianic title, "Son of man," is virtually confined to the Gospels. Though it must certainly have been known to the authors of the New Testament Epistles, they could not bring themselves to use it. And this, too, cannot be an accident. On the other hand, there are essential elements of the Pauline Christology which can be explained as the interpretation or "theologization" of the Son-of-man sayings of Jesus.

We will again epitomize the negative result of our investigations up to this point: the *Sitz im Leben* and the original source of the Gospel tradition were neither mission preaching nor the communal instruction of the primitive church.

It is now high time to enter upon the positive aspects of our problem. And only one possible answer remains, even if it demands an extended analysis, namely: the Gospel tradition belongs to a category which is *sui generis* and, to put the matter concisely, it has its own setting. It is a conclusion which has been forcing itself upon us with ever-growing insistence. It is true that even when we have recognized this, we are still at the outset of our task. Yet to have seen this much enables us to break through the fetters which arise from a one-sided application of the form-critical method.

It is not incompatible with insistence on the unique character of the primitive Christian message, and hence of the Gospel tradition, to draw attention to analogies from the milieu in which this Gospel tradition arose. Strangely, these have been insufficiently heeded hitherto. Preaching and instruction were commonplaces alike in Palestinian Judaism and in the Jewish Diaspora of the Mediterranean world, even though their character was far less intense than in the early church. But no real student of Judaism in the Hellenistic age would for one moment imagine that their authoritative or "holy" words originated from preaching or from instruction of the community or from controversy with the surrounding world.

As regards the writings of the Old Testament, their literary content was already fixed at this period. Hence in this case there could be no question of any oral tradition. But side by side with the text of the Old Testament there existed an extensive and important complex of tradition. This was the so-called Sayings of the Fathers, that comprehensive exposition and elaboration of the Law which was carefully handed on from generation to generation and finally found its literary embodiment in the Mishnah *ca.* A.D. 200. In this case we have indeed an authoritative "holy" tradition which was thought ultimately to derive from the revelation of Yahweh to Moses on Mount Sinai.

As regards the nature of this Jewish tradition and its transmission, we are, as it happens, relatively well-informed.[8] But what justifies us in drawing from it a number of conclusions relating to primitive Christianity is the fact that the terminology used of the Jewish process of tradition reappears in the New Testament. It appears here, indeed, in Greek translation, but it is easily recognizable. But we must add at the outset—to guard ourselves from conveying the misleading impression of putting the Gospel tradition on the same level as the Jewish interpretation of the Law— that we are here concerned only with the formal side of the process of tradition and not directly with its content as such.

[8]E.g., W. Bacher, *Tradition und Tradenten in den Schulen Palästinas und Babyloniens* (1914); G. Kittel, *Die Probleme des palästinischen Spätjudentums und das Urchristentum* (1926), pp. 7 ff., 63–70; O. Cullmann, *Die Tradition als exegetisches, historisches und theologisches Problem* (1954), pp. 12 ff.

Παραλαμβάνειν, "take over," Hebrew *qibbēl,* denotes the imprinting of a tradition of doctrine with which one had been entrusted, while παραδιδόναι, "hand over," Hebrew *māsar,* is used of its commitment to a particular pupil. The situation as here conceived is not the vague diffusion of narratives, sagas, or anecdotes, as we find in folklore, but the rigidly controlled transmission of matter from one who has the mastery of it to another who has been specially chosen to learn it. The bearer of the tradition and the teacher *(rabbi)* watched over its memorizing by his approved pupils *(talmīd)* and what was passed on in this way was, in the matter both of content and form, a fixed body of material. Especially was this so as regards the Halachic material of the Mishnah tradition, that is, as regards its specially important "holy" constituent. The ideal pupil was one who never lost one iota of the tradition. That variations in the material took place in the process of tradition for psychological reasons is obvious, and this circumstance enables us to investigate the development of the tradition from another angle. For however great its receptive capacities, even an Oriental mind is not a tape recorder.

From the circumstances that the rabbinic tradition was strictly controlled and its transmission regulated by firmly established laws—a fact bound up with the conception of the transmitted material as holy word—it follows that the oral tradition was esoteric, and this not in the sense that it was treasured as a dark secret, but that it was not entrusted to everyone nor was it at everyone's disposal to use as he wished.

All this means, therefore, that in New Testament times the specifically Jewish tradition, at any rate, was not possessed and shaped by an unlimited and undefined anonymous multitude. The people or the synagogue community were, of course, instructed in the Scriptures and in the tradition of the law, but such instruction never made a community as such bearers of the tradition. On the contrary, those who performed this task were an exactly defined group within the community.

From this point we can now explain, or at least throw light on, the New Testament conception of παράδοσις, "tradition." For it has been one of the defects of form criticism, as it has been employed hitherto, that all too little notice has been taken of the relevant analogies in the Palestinian conception of tradition.

Let us, then, return to the New Testament. There is a characteristic passage in Paul which is relevant in this connection. He writes: "Finally, brethren, we beseech and exhort you in the Lord Jesus, that as you learned from us [i.e., the tradition] how you ought to live and to please God, just as you are doing, you do so more and more" (1 Thess. 4:1). Here the apostle is using the terminology to which we have already referred: the community has received a tradition through his mediation. But what sort of a tradition? Examination of the use of similar expressions elsewhere in Paul justifies us in assuming that they were words of Jesus about the nature of discipleship and the mode of life to be followed by the brethren.

To be brief, I will merely state one of the conclusions which follow from a large body of evidence. Paul was himself the bearer of the Gospel tradition, that is, he carefully took it over and gave it shape. In the long autobiographical passage at the beginning of the Epistle to the Galatians he says that he spent three years in Arabia after his conversion and then went to Jerusalem and visited Peter, with whom he stayed fifteen days. It is reasonable to conclude that his chief concern in these weeks was not theological discussions or ecclesiastical projects, but something which was a precondition of the fulfillment of his apostolic work, namely that Peter should test whether he, Paul, during his term of preparation, had really made the tradition of the words and deeds of Jesus his own, in the form, that is, which these words and deeds had assumed by that date. For in the Pauline Epistles we see that the apostle is dependent on an overmastering tradition, and this must have been mainly the Gospel tradition in its own individuality. If Paul, like the other writers of the New Testament Epistles, usually refrains from expressly quoting this tradition—and this reticence, of which we still have to speak, is certainly intentional—yet in certain specially important places he makes it clear that he has access to the verbal tradition, e.g., in the passage where he solemnly introduces as a quotation the Words of Institution at the Last Supper (1 Cor. 11:23–25). The way in which Paul handles such a quotation shows that the words of the tradition did not, in fact, normally find a place in a letter.

Now just because Paul was in a special way the bearer of the tradition of the words and deeds of Jesus, he could consider himself as on a level with the other apostles, and especially with the Twelve. For the chief obligations of the apostles included not only preaching and the oversight of the communities, but also the safekeeping and committal to trustworthy persons of the words and deeds of Jesus, that is of the Gospel tradition. We can see this especially clearly from certain passages in the Lucan writings. In Acts 6 the activity of the apostles is described with some exactness: "It is not right that we should give up preaching the word of God to serve tables" (6:2). Hence seven collaborators were selected for the latter task, while the apostles devoted themselves to prayer and the "service" (διακονία) of the "word." Wherein this service consisted, and that it was not regarded as being primarily preaching, follows from the phrase here employed: λόγος τοῦ θεοῦ, the "word of

God." We may also recall the prologue to Luke's Gospel, which comes from the same writer as Acts. Here we read of the events of the life of Jesus, "just as they were delivered to us [we may note the *terminus technicus*] by those who from the beginning were eyewitnesses and ministers (ὑπηρέται) of the word" (Luke 1:2). The words and deeds of Jesus are a holy word, comparable with that of the Old Testament, and the handing down of this precious material is entrusted to special persons. And just for this reason it was so important, when the twelfth place in the circle of the disciples had become vacant through the fall and death of Judas Iscariot and had to be filled again, to find someone who was—as we read—"one of the men who have accompanied us [i.e., with the Twelve] during all the time that the Lord Jesus went in and out among us, beginning from the baptism of John until the day when he was taken up from us—one of these men must become with us a witness to his resurrection" (Acts 1:21–22). Hence to be an apostle or witness of the resurrection it was not sufficient to have met the risen Christ, but that person had to possess such a living impression of the life and work of Jesus as to make him qualified to transmit the holy tradition of the words and deeds of Jesus.

Now can we find in the most primitive Christianity any *Sitz im Leben* of such a special "holy" tradition about Jesus? We are helped in answering this question if we consider the literary genus of this tradition which precedes the Gospels in their definitive written form. Comparison with the style of the prophetic discourses of the Old Testament, on the one hand, and with the rabbinic material, on the other, suggests that the tradition was recited, and, since the tradition was not esoteric in the narrower sense, that it was recited not exclusively to hearers who were destined to become future transmitters of the tradition.

But as soon as ever one reflects on the character of this Christian tradition as holy word, as the word of God, and as something parallel to the holy writings of the Old Testament, the very smallest knowledge of religious life in Palestine forces the conclusion that the words and deeds of Jesus were not just improvised, that there was no question of freely narrating or of inventing, even when the speaker was possessed by the Spirit. On the contrary, the strict laws relating to holy tradition will have prevailed from the outset and determined both what was uttered and what was transmitted, in spite of the fact that in points of detail variations could not but appear and, indeed, did appear.

But where, we may ask, was this traditional material uttered or recited? Here too we can give the answer. It would evidently have been in the assemblies of the community. We must again picture in our minds analogies drawn from the use of the sacred books of the Old Testament in Judaism. It is significant that the original New Testament designation for the Gospel tradition was not εὐαγγελίον—this word stands for its missionary appeal—but λόγος and λόγος θεοῦ—terms which correspond with the names current in Judaism for "Holy Scripture."[9] The words of Jesus and the reports of his deeds and his life, although originally transmitted by word of mouth, were conceived from a very early date to be the New Torah, and hence as the word of God of the new, eschatological covenant.

Now we know from the accounts in Acts that the original Jerusalem community took part in the services in the Temple and in the synagogues, and they did so, we may conclude, for the sake of the prayers and Bible readings.

[9]Cf. λέγω, λόγος, in Gerhard Kittel, ed., *Theological Dictionary of the New Testament,* trans. G. W. Bromiley (Grand Rapids: Eerdman's, 1964–), vol. 4. Hereafter cited as Kittel.

But besides this public worship, the community which believed in the risen Lord gathered in a closer circle—first in the upper room and soon also in private houses—for the breaking of bread, for prayer, and for instruction by the apostles, δ'λδαχὴ τῶν ἀποστόλων, which took place in the presence of the whole community (Acts 2:42). In view of such participation in the Jewish worship, it is natural to regard the apostles' instruction as being in the first place the recounting of the words and deeds of Jesus, as the complement to the sacred word of the Old Testament which the community had already heard. Indeed, it would have been not only its complement, but also its fulfillment. As in the synagogue, exposition followed the recitation, and of this exposition we have some indications in the New Testament Epistles.

Here we have the reason why the words and deeds of Jesus were probably never quoted verbally in the missionary preaching and only on rare occasions in the community instruction. The tradition which was recited was holy and hence, in contrast to present-day practice, was not readily mentioned by word of mouth. Mission preaching, indeed, pointed and led to it. The instruction in the community presupposed it and linked itself up with it. But in its verbal form and in its function in the community it was *sui generis.*

From this point we can gain light on the transmission of the tradition in the early church and on the process of its literary fixation. In view of the fact that the recitation of the tradition about Jesus as the sacred word of the New Covenant was an essential constituent in Christian public worship, it is certain that the need for authorized transmitters of this tradition became greater as the Christian church itself grew and its communities increased in number. This need must have contributed fundamentally to the growth of the Christian ministry. It was the same set of circumstances which, again in analogy with the Old Testament, led to the written fixation of the text at a comparatively early date. In this process it was the words of Jesus which were brought together first, just as in Judaism special importance was attached to the Sayings of the Fathers. The earliest step away from the original exclusiveness of the holy tradition is the Gospel of Luke which already places the words and deeds of Jesus in a literary and apologetic framework.

But to fully understand the origin of the Gospel tradition we must go back further still. How can we explain the fact that in the first age of the church the tradition about Jesus already possessed its special character as holy word? The answer must be that this tradition, *qua* tradition, was derived from none other than Jesus. Hence our thesis is that the beginning of the Gospel tradition lies with Jesus himself.

In the Gospels we are shown very clearly that Jesus was a teacher, and especially in his relation to his disciples.[10] This means more than his mere preaching in their presence. He gave them instruction, and in this we are reminded, *mutatis mutandis*, of the method of the Jewish rabbi. And this implies that Jesus made his disciples, and above all the Twelve, learn, and furthermore that he made them learn by heart.

And, if we view the matter from the other side, it is also evident that some of the main portions of Jesus' sayings in the Gospels are formulated so as to be suited to transmission and memorization. Here too we can make comparisons with the stylistic laws of the sacred tradition of the Jews, though we must not overlook the differences. Of

[10]Cf. K. H. Rengstorf, διδάσκαλος, in Kittel, vol. 2; William Manson, *Jesus the Messiah* (London: Hodder & Stoughton, 1943), pp. 51 ff.

the Lord's Prayer it was expressly said that Jesus taught his disciples this (Luke 11:1 f.; cf. Matt. 6:9). But, apart from this, many of the words of Jesus are in such a form that not only is it possible to hear the echoes of the Aramaic original, but also to deduce that they were carefully formulated so as to be apt for transmission.[11] We may take the case of the parable of the building of the house with which the Sermon on the Mount in the First Gospel concludes: "Every one then who hears these words of mine and does them will be like a wise man who built his house upon the rock; and the rain fell, and the floods came, and the winds blew and beat upon that house, but it did not fall, because it had been founded on the rock. And every one who hears these words of mine and does not do them will be like a foolish man who built his house upon the sand; and the rain fell, and the floods came, and the winds blew and beat against that house, and it fell; and great was the fall of it" (Matt. 7:24–27).

In accord with this is the fact that even after the translation of the tradition into Greek, certain words of Jesus were preserved in their original Aramaic form, as for instance *Talitha qūm* (RSV *Taľitha cu'mi*), "Little girl, I say to you, arise," in the narrative of the awakening of Jairus's daughter (Mark 5:41). It is not here a case of the use of magical words in acts of healing in the primitive community. What we have are formulas which were treasured in the memory for the sake of Jesus, and this because they came from him and not for any miraculous power they might possess.

The preaching of Jesus before the Palestinian crowds was revelation, the announcement of a divine secret, μυστήριον.

---

[11] C. F. Burney, *The Poetry of Our Lord* (London: Oxford University Press, 1925); Matthew Black, *An Aramaic Approach to the Gospels and Acts* (London: Oxford University Press, 1946), pp. 105 ff.

We must think of the disciples, in their relation to this message, as sitting at Jesus' feet, partly in order to hear once again the words and to get to know them by heart, partly that they might be instructed in their meaning as, e.g. (in the matter of method), in Mark 4:10: "And when he was alone, those who were about him with the twelve asked him concerning the parables." In this way they were taught the destiny of the Son of man and the conditions of following after him, matters which in Jesus' lifetime were intended for a more esoteric and narrower circle of disciples (cf. John 16:1 ff.).

In modern times such a picture of the origins of the Gospel tradition as the following is often met with: the preaching of Jesus, who was possessed by the prophetic Spirit, was free and without restraint. Some of this preaching survived with more or less verbal accuracy in the memories of his hearers. Besides, it was the custom in the primitive church to preach freely and without restraint, and in this process sayings and narratives were created and invented. And then from this extensive body of material the evangelists or their predecessors made a well-considered selection. But this romantic picture has no relation to reality. On the contrary, it is probable both that from Jesus' own days the material was far more strictly limited and also that it was handed down in a far more rigid and fixed form. One indication of this is the very limited extent of the extra-canonical tradition of Jesus. It is evident that Jesus did not preach indiscriminately nor continually, but that he imposed certain limitations on his preaching as he did in the case of his miracles. And what was essential to his message he taught his disciples, that is, he made them learn it by heart. Doubtless there are small parts of it which have fallen by the way, but we may well ask whether the bulk of it is not preserved in our Gospels. Such a statement as John 21:25 is clearly an exaggeration.

Along this road we can advance still farther. We can inquire whether the tradition of Jesus' deeds cannot also be traced back in its beginnings to Jesus himself. Naturally this cannot apply to the passion narratives, which form a unit apart, with their own problems. But there are indications in connection, e.g., with the miracles of the feeding (Mark 8:19–21), which lead to the conclusion that Jesus also spoke with his disciples about deeds and their significance. We may also compare the reply to the Baptist on the subject of miracles (Mark 11:4 f.). And it is probable that the kernel of the narratives of the baptism and the temptations are to be derived from Jesus' teaching in the circle of his disciples.

The account of the anointing at Bethany (Mark 14:3–9) concludes with a saying of Jesus about the woman with the alabaster vessel and her gracious act: "And truly, I say to you, wherever the gospel is preached in the whole world, what she has done will be told in memory of her." This remark at the end of the narrative is generally regarded as a secondary addition from the days of the primitive church. But the question arises whether the thought expressed in the passage is necessarily incompatible with the situation and the intention of Jesus, either in the actual setting here given to it or some other of a similar kind. That Jesus reckoned with an intervening epoch between his death and the parousia, that is, with the epoch of the church, appears to me a necessary consequence of the institution of the Lord's Supper. The sacrament is intended as a symbolic action which derives its meaning from its relation to the church. But is it possible to conceive of any such action in the intention of Jesus without the complement of the word? Hence we must seriously ask whether Jesus did not reckon with the announcement of the Good News in the epoch of the church, and whether he did not, in view of this preaching, transmit to his disciples a λόγος whose outlines were already defined. There is the duality of word and action both with Jesus and in the church. Between the deeds of Jesus and the sacramental action of the church there exists an ascertainable connection. Should not a like connection also exist between the preaching of Jesus and the tradition of the words and deeds of Jesus in the church? I therefore make bold to conjecture that Jesus reckoned with what we may call the recital of the Gospel tradition in the epoch between his death and the parousia.

In asserting this we are naturally not saying either that the Gospel tradition existed from the very first in its settled form as we find it in the synoptic tradition, or that it can be traced back to Jesus in its definitive shape. It is self-evident that the molding of the tradition—e.g., by the collecting and grouping of individual pericopes, through its transformations and also through its additions—came about gradually in the life of the primitive church. The essential point is that the outlines, that is, the beginnings of the proper genus of the tradition of the words and deeds of Jesus, were memorized and recited as holy word. We should be inclined to trace these outlines back to Jesus' activity as a teacher in the circle of his disciples. Another consequence of such considerations is that we reach a more positive attitude to the question whether the essential constituents of the Christology and ethics, as we now have them in the bulk of the tradition, may not go back to Jesus himself.

Along these lines we also reach vantage points from which to judge the Johannine tradition. It is clear that the development of the material in this Gospel took place in accordance with rules which in some ways differed from those which controlled the synoptic material. It is a characteristic of the Johannine mode of presentation that the words and deeds of Jesus are, so to speak, commented on, that they became the object of "meditations." Here too I should incline to the view that the Gospel of John rests on an independent line of tradition, which had its original starting point in the activity of Jesus, and which then ran parallel with the synoptic line of tradition. And here the starting point is to be found in the discourses and "meditations" of Jesus in the circle of his disciples, such as certainly took place side by side with the instruction of the disciples proper, with its more rigid forms. Such a view is not incompatible with this line of tradition having also undergone a long and complex development.

But in the last resort the solution given to the whole problem of the Gospel tradition depends on the inquirer's attitude to the problem of the messianic self-consciousness. Here again we find that this is the central question for the interpretation of the New Testament and the point at which the ways divide.

If we take in all seriousness the position that Jesus regarded himself in some way as the Messiah and that as a result of this he also drew the consequences of a fully developed messianic system of ideas,[12] then we need not be surprised if Jesus was conscious of himself as the bearer of revelation, as the bringer of the new Law, and as a teacher.[13] Granted the messianic consciousness, then the circle of the disciples formed the kernel of the corresponding eschatological community. In view of the Old Testament

[12]Cf. Manson, *Jesus the Messiah*, pp. 97 f.
[13]William D. Davies, *Torah in the Messianic Age and/or the Age to Come* (Lancaster, Pa.: Society of Biblical Literature and Exegesis, 1952), pp. 90 ff.; idem, *The Setting of the Sermon on the Mount* (New York: Cambridge University Press, 1964), pp. 109 ff.

background and the messianic hopes of the Jews, we can legitimately assume that Jesus entrusted to his disciples, and hence to the eschatological people of God, an already formulated holy word for it to transmit, and that this was the starting point of a tradition. For if we assume the messianic consciousness, then Jesus must also have spoken about the significance of his person and the rules for the conduct of life in the messianic community. In this particular matter the writings from the Dead Sea at least point the way.

In modern handbooks on the theology of the New Testament the appearance and proclamation of Jesus are sometimes treated as prolegomena.[14] So regarded, Jesus of Nazareth belongs to the history of later Judaism. Christianity—that is, faith in Jesus as Messiah and redeemer—first arose in the primitive community after the resurrection and hence is to be treated as a subject separate from the preaching of Jesus. Over against this view, the considerations which have just been urged lead us back to the "classical" method of interpretation. The belief in Christ is to be found already in the words and deeds of Jesus just because Jesus regarded himself as the Messiah. The faith of the primitive church had its origin in what Jesus proclaimed and set forth in symbolic form. One of the preconditions of this has already been established: it was owing to the tradition of the deeds and words of Jesus which began from Jesus himself that the primitive church had the basis for its faith. This gives us a profitable starting point from which to compare our four Gospels, both among themselves and also with the rest of the New Testament writings, as the expression of the faith of the first Christian generations.

[14]Rudolf Bultmann, *Theology of the New Testament*, trans. Kendrick Grobel (2 vols.; New York: Charles Scribner's Sons, 1951–55).

When we reckon with the fact that Jesus is the founder of the Gospel tradition, both as to its essence and its original starting point, we arrive naturally at a synthesis which is again classical and see in the "Gospel of Jesus Christ" (εὐαγγέλιον Ἰησοῦ Χριστοῦ, cf. Mark 1:1) both the Good News brought by Jesus Christ (subjective genitive) and the Good News about Jesus Christ (objective genitive). By simply tracing their descent we find the two lines here united in the person and work of Jesus.

We have here attempted to give an answer to the question as to the origin of the Gospel tradition. We must seek its origin ultimately in Jesus and his messianic self-consciousness. Jesus is not only the object of a later faith, which on its side gave rise to the growth of oral and also written tradition, but, as Messiah and teacher, Jesus is the object and subject of a tradition of authoritative and holy words which he himself created and entrusted to his disciples for its later transmission in the epoch between his death and the parousia.

II. The Mythological Background
of New Testament Christology

About half a century ago it was believed that a key had been found to the main questions of the New Testament. The opinion prevailed among more advanced scholars that primitive Christianity had been largely influenced by mystery cults of the Hellenistic age. It was supposed that the person and life of Christ were molded, in the writings of the New Testament, after those of Eastern and Greek heroes or gods. It was then that W. Bousset wrote his acute and learned book *Kyrios Christos,* where the Christology of the primitive church was explained by supposing that mythological elements from the religions in the Mediterranean world had been condensing around the traditions about the person of Christ. This point of view cannot, in its entirety, be maintained any longer, because it seems to be, in spite of its learned argumentation, a construction which, when all is said and done, merely raises questions instead of answering them.

Nowadays, scholars of Christology, if they are anxious to isolate not only the specific outlines of primitive Christianity, but also its genetic relation to Judaism, can, of course, consider Bousset's ideas to be a temporary tendency in New Testament study. There is, however, an important factor which, apart from the relativity that is always to be found in the conception of a scholar or of a group of scholars, gives one the feeling of being on solid ground. This is that the writings of the New Testament bear such clear witness to the connection of primitive Christianity with the Old Testament and the religious history of Israel, on the one hand, and with Palestinian Judaism, on the other. If one wishes to deal with the forms and contents of New Testament Christology, it seems to be necessary to return to the elements of Jewish Messianism.

In studies of the Old Testament and of later Judaism there has been a keen interest in the figure of the Messiah and of its place in eschatology. The importance of the annual cycle of worship for the formation of the religious conceptions of the Jewish people has often been pointed out. Following on this it is apparent that the king, in pre-exilic times, held a central position in the Israelite cult. He represented God to the people and the people to God. Because of his religious function as a mediator, it was around his person that many of the ideas of salvation belonging to all cult and to all belief crystallized. To the extent to which the figure of an ideal king and the conceptions bound up with this figure were projected into the future—a procedure to which the exile itself and the conditions which it brought to the people undoubtedly contributed—there grew up the eschatological hope, the waiting for a king of the Davidic dynasty who would restore, after a period of humiliation and visitation, the Palestinian kingship, and reign over it in a time of victory and peace, justice and security. This king for whom the people were waiting was called the Messiah. In fact the faith in an ideal king was in no way confined to Israel or to the peoples of the ancient Near East, but it cannot be denied that these conceptions have been formed, in the Old Testament and in later Judaism, in quite a special way. It is necessary, therefore, to analyze the forms of this messianic hope, and in so doing one will realize that there is a natural connection between belief in the Messiah and belief in God. Life, justice, salvation to be brought by the Messiah, the judgment held by him and the people gathered by him—all these are fundamental conceptions of the Israelite faith which occur constantly in Old Testament texts. The Messiah is the representative of God, sent by him in order to mediate and to carry into effect the final justification and beatitude of mankind. As Yahweh is the living God, life will flourish in all its fullness in the reign of the Messiah. The hope of a paradise arises from the belief in a perfect life. And because God has chosen for his purposes a nation, the people gathered and led by the Messiah will show themselves to be worthy of this election by living up to the claims of obedience and perfection which God has set up. At the same time, however, the people will share in the divine mercy and blessing which are a logical result of the election. The promises, which, with their various pictures and colors, give a characteristic mark to the prophetic books of the Old Testament, will reach their fulfillment, but this cannot happen until a presumption has been realized, and this is that the powers, the nations, and the individuals inimical to Yahweh are judged and doomed.

When accounting for the messianic hopes of the Jewish people in postexilic and New Testament times, scholars have customarily presupposed two different kinds of savior. They have distinguished sharply between the immanent and anthropomorphic national king Messiah and the transcendent Son of man borne on heavenly clouds, and they have treated them as representing thoroughly different features. That is to say the roots of the latter idea have been sought exclusively in Iranian eschatology, which in various ways, especially during the exile, could have influenced Jewish religious conceptions. But in making such a supposition one has to ask oneself—as, for example, when dealing with Jewish belief in the resurrection of the dead—if it is possible to postulate influences from other peoples and other religions without making clear such points of contact within

Jewish belief as necessarily must have existed before any influence from outside could have gained ground within Judaism. A more profound investigation of the texts shows that the distinction between the immanent Messiah and the transcendent Son of man is not absolutely clear-cut. There are, on the contrary, transcendent features to be found in the national type of Messiah characteristic of the Psalms of Solomon and the Testaments of the Twelve Patriarchs, while the Son of man of the First Book of Enoch or of the Apocalypses of Baruch and Ezra is depicted in such a manner that several details can be called messianic in a stricter sense. When reading about the enthronement of the priestly Messiah in the Testament of Levi (chaps. viii and xviii), one becomes aware that the earthly, immanent perspective passes into a heavenly and cosmic one, just as, in all worship, the wall between heaven and earth tends to be broken down.

It seems, therefore, to be reasonable to assume—though it cannot be demonstrated here in detail—that the difference between the Messiah and the Son of man is not only due to influences from abroad in the latter case, but that there have been tendencies leading to a differentiation of eschatological conceptions within postexilic Jewish religion. This differentiation takes its departure from the two aspects which are to be seen already in preexilic cult and eschatology: the immanent and the transcendent. The same duality is to some extent characteristic also of the idea of a coming Messiah from the very beginning of this conception. This more advanced process of differentiation has its place in the spiritual life of postexilic Judaism with its different currents of piety. There was on the one side a realistic nationalism, the eschatological hope of which centered around the ideal king and the political liberator. This savior was supposed to effect, as regards the religious life of the people, a cleansing and intensification of the national worship which was concentrated in Jerusalem, though the growing institution of the synagogues led to a certain decentralization of ordinary worship. Quite the same tendency is to be detected in the priestly aspirations of the sectarians who in New Testament times were centered about the western shore of the Dead Sea. On the other side there were circles, probably localized chiefly in Galilee, in which apocalyptic ideas, together with a transcendental understanding of eschatology, were developed. There the figure of the heavenly Son of man was evolved together with the related belief in the universality of salvation, which was lacking in the conception of a national Messiah. Thus, it is probable that certain ideas incorporated in the conceptions of the Son of man have evolved from the belief in a heavenly savior which, having originated in ancient Persia, spread over the countries of the Near East; but nevertheless it seems to be not impossible to suppose that the two figures, the Messiah and the Son of man, still had so much in common in New Testament times that Jews belonging to different opinions were aware of the fact that they expected the same savior, whether they spoke of the Messiah-to-come or of the Son of man.

We shall not deal with details of the messianic hope of the Jewish people. It is, however, obvious that it has grown up from ideas belonging to Israelite kingship. But, in order to underline an important point of view, why is it necessary, even for the New Testament scholar, to work out not only the connections of Christology with the messianic conceptions of Judaism, but also the lines from these conceptions backward to preexilic kingship? The answer lies in the acquisition, by this method, of the key to the pictorial language, to the metaphors and thus to the ideas belonging to the messianic hope, and, having understood the language, we can proceed to the understanding of the religious thoughts. Every effort to express experiences belonging to the realm of faith is dependent on metaphorical language; word pictures are used as garments with which the thoughts are clothed. But these pictures are derived from realities which have been experienced visually. As to religious metaphors, they are drawn to a large extent from the cult and from its different rites, an important function of which is to make visible the invisible. During the last decades Old Testament scholars have laid stress upon the role of the king in the rites belonging to the yearly cycle of festivals in the religious and national life of Israel, and they have investigated ritual patterns and their substance, thus laying a valuable foundation for the understanding of the vocabulary used to express different lines of thought in eschatology and especially in the messianic hope. There are of course fluctuations in terminology and in the application of pictures and metaphors, and all alterations have to be analyzed. But in the main there is a very conservative tendency in the pictorial language and in the metaphors, and alterations of thought are mostly expressed by new combinations of motifs. When dealing with such a complex of religious ideas as the messianic hope, one has to take into consideration a double problem: what motifs are used to express the belief in a Messiah, and what ideas are expressed by the various motifs employed?

Let us return for a moment to some dominating features in the conceptions of the Messiah. The savior-to-come is described as a king, a term which is meant both to express a political reality and also, as far as transcendent events are concerned, to have a metaphorical content. The kingship of the Messiah helps to underline his majesty and power, but there are even more important associations to be found in the term. It is obvious that a king has a kingdom, a dominion where he reigns and where he realizes his intentions. Therefore there exists a fundamental relation between the Messiah and the kingdom of God. For even if in some parts of later Jewish literature the Messiah is not mentioned in texts dealing with eschatology, while Yahweh himself appears as the final king, it has to be remembered that there is in no way a rivalry between Yahweh and his Messiah, but that the latter is always regarded as the visible representative of God, and that he reigns endowed with divine authority. The kingdom, on the other hand, has its raison d'être because of the people living within its borders. The king reigning over a people has to exercise his authority in such a way that he furthers the welfare of his subjects. The obligations of the governing and the governed are reciprocal. This is so also in the kingdom of the Messiah. He and the people of God are inseparable: the Messiah redeeming his people in order to procure new conditions of life, the people serving their king in righteousness and thus glorifying him.

The idea of the king is only one of the many motifs bound up with Jewish messianism, but it is sufficient to analyze one such motif and its background in Israelite history and worship in order to receive an impression of the continuity which is characteristic of religious terms and conceptions in the Old Testament and in later Judaism. It is certainly not out of the way to speak of the history of the people of God even on the spiritual level. The Israelite kingship, the sociological structure of the Israelites, their religious life, condensed in holy scriptures, their worship and rites, all these are elements in a long process which—from the point of view of the New Testament—can be characterized as a preparation or prefiguration, a time of forming and molding of the terms and metaphors and thoughts, the existence of which was a necessary condition for the proclamation of the gospel by Jesus and for the belief of the church from its very beginning. In this process a dominating place is occupied by messianology, which covers the evolution from the Davidic kingdom to the very point where Christology begins. But in order to catch the nuances of Christology—as well as of other New Testament ideas—it is necessary first to investigate the previous history of the "motifs," especially in Jewish messianology.

There are reflections of the same kind to be made when dealing with the figure of the Son of man. In Daniel 7 his appearance is described in terms drawn from the royal enthronement. Behind the Son of man, as well as behind the Messiah, there is the idea of the king. But in addition, modern commentators on Daniel 7 have discussed the question whether the heavenly savior is to be interpreted as a symbol of the saved people or as an individual ruler. Now there is a certain ambiguity in the text itself. In the description of the vision (vv. 13 f.), the individual traits prevail, while in the following comment a collective sense is stressed (v. 28). It has been justly remarked that there need not be an absolute antithesis between the two interpretations. In the figure of the Son of man, individual and collective features are to be found beside each other, and this is not an accidental conjunction, but is due to traditional ideas. In ancient Israel—as well as elsewhere in the ancient Near East—the king was thought of as summing up and representing the people. That is why it is not surprising to find composite traits in the figure of the Son of man, and that is the case also in other apocalyptic writings in later Judaism. The clue to this ambiguity lies again in the fact that the king and his people, as well as the savior and the saved community, are indissoluble.

As we have already said, the figure and thus the term of the Son of man express in a higher degree than those of the Messiah the notion of universality which evidently, in spite of all national limitations, existed even in Israelite conceptions of the king and the chosen people. But in Jewish apocalyptics the Son of man has a bearing not only upon the people of Israel, but upon mankind; his reign is not confined to a flourishing Palestine, but comprises a new world.

Closely connected with the function of king was that of high priest. This was so from the time when the Davidic king was also the highest sacral official of the people, the leader of the cult performed in the temple. It is a characteristic fact that the robe of the high priest in the postexilic period was that of the king in preexilic times, and that the high priest was inaugurated into his office, at any rate during the first centuries of its existence, by anointing. Therefore it is rather natural that the Messiah-to-come is described also as the ideal high priest. A special importance was given to this idea when the Hasmonaean Dynasty was reigning in Palestine. Its members belonged to a priestly family and were therefore lacking in the royal qualifications restricted to the Davidic family. This resulted in the priesthood of the Messiah being underlined in accounts from that time of the eschatological events. There are striking examples in the Testaments of the Twelve Patriarchs, especially in that of Levi. Also in the Damascus Document, as well as in the Dead Sea Scrolls, the importance of the ideas connected with the eschatological priesthood is evident. The principal task of the priestly Messiah will be the establishment of definite and perfect temple worship. After the fall of Jerusalem and of the Herodean temple, there are to be found in Jewish prayers supplications that God might send his Messiah to restore the temple and its worship. This association of the person of the Messiah with the temple of Jerusalem and with the cult performed there is in no way strange. On the contrary an important fact is here expressed. Cult is the visible form in which the relation between God and mankind takes shape. The duty of the priest, and especially of the high priest, is to be responsible for this cult and to present, on behalf of the people, the offerings prescribed by God himself, all that is necessary in order to eliminate the disorder in the relation between God and man caused by the guilt of man. The person of the Messiah stands as a mediator, restorer, and savior at the very point where the confrontation of man with God becomes most evident.

There is one more function of office of the Messiah which ought to be mentioned in addition to the two discussed hitherto. Even in this case it is possible to establish historical relations to the other ones from far remote times. This function is the prophetic one. When Josephus wanted to pay homage to the memory of the great Hasmonaean prince John Hyrcanus, he characterized him as ruler (i.e., king), high priest, and prophet, endowed by God with these three charges.[1] In the Testament of Levi (chap. viii) there is another proof of the combinations of the three offices in the person of the Messiah. There are of course other functions to be detected in the descriptions of the Messiah, but there is no doubt that the three mentioned are the most important ones. If the Messiah is a prophet or *the* prophet who sums up and fulfills the work of all prophets who have come before, that means that he is a messenger sent to mankind from God in order to let them know and to interpret to them in a final way the will of God, which otherwise is hidden to their minds. The prophet acts by demonstrating in words and deeds. In ancient Israel the functions of the prophets were in some respects closely connected to the kingship as well as to the priesthood, and

[1] Josephus *Antiquities* 13. 299; *Bell.* 1. 68.

these offices had several traits in common. Prophecy is, for instance, based on the possession of the divine spirit. The same spirit, conveyed by anointing, is, however, the attribute of the king and later on of the high priest. It is the same with the law, which was proclaimed by the king and also by the prophet—we need only think of Moses and of the role attributed to him in later Judaism. The Messiah will thus be equipped with the spirit, the abundance of which is one of the signs of the coming age, and he will also promulgate the new or rather the definite law, and that means the regulating of human relations and of human conditions of life according to the will of God.

In Jewish messianology in New Testament times, there are thus to be found an abundant number of motifs—of which only a few have been mentioned here—and these motifs can all be traced back to concrete features in the political or religious life of the Jewish people, and one has always to remember that there were no strict borders between the national and the sacral sphere. The expectation of the messianic age was at a high pitch in the time of the Herods, which was also that of the Roman occupation. But at the same time the messianic hope was a disparate phenomenon, two different forms of which were the idea of the national Messiah and that of the Son of man. It is to be noted that the different conceptions of the Messiah as they meet in various situations or texts are formed by varying combinations of metaphors or motifs which were traditional. It seems that the conception which was adopted to a greater extent by the Jewish population in New Testament times was that of the specifically national Messiah, which was, however, after the serious adversities and the bitter disappointments of the first and the second centuries A.D., to fade away. Quite as important as the combinations of traditional elements in the different forms of the messianic hope in Jewish eschatology is the very existence of these elements—at least it seems so from the point of view of the New Testament scholar. For he may be interested not so much in the actual result of those Jewish combinations as in the elements and motifs, in their meaning and in their ability to express religious ideas. Therefore it appears to be an attractive task to investigate the history of these elements and thus to penetrate into their meaning and into their associations with central points in the religious life of the Jewish people: the idea of God, the Scriptures, the temple cult, the ideas of election and of the covenant, and, finally, the hope of salvation.

When Jesus proclaimed his gospel he did not preach abstract religious or moral thoughts, but presented himself as the center of the coming kingdom of God. By means of the metaphorical language and of the traditional symbols which he used in his words and his deeds, he proclaimed, if his listeners were willing to understand, that he was no less a person than the Messiah. By his own activity he laid the ground for the faith, i.e., for the christological belief, of the church which was to grow up after his death and resurrection. The center in all Christology is Jesus Christ, not only because he is the object of the theological and dogmatic thinking of the primitive Church, but, above all, because he himself has created Christology in its very kernel. For to the question, "What manner of man was Jesus?" we feel obliged to answer not only, "He was the Messiah"—which is an answer of faith—but also, "He thought himself to be the Messiah"—a reply which emerges from the study of the texts. This is not the place to enter into a discussion of the messianic consciousness of Jesus; we only want to point out that the way in which Jesus is described in the Gospels cannot be finally explained without assuming a messianic conception in the mind of Jesus himself. For

by means of the metaphors and symbols which Jesus used
—and which in the main at least were not combined with
his person secondarily, i.e., after his death and in the faith
of the Christian Church—we can get an insight into the
purpose of his activity and thus into his self-consciousness.
Neither is it necessary to demonstrate here the Palestinian
and Old Testament background of the terms and symbols
used by Jesus. As to the formal side of his preaching and
acting, he was deeply rooted in the milieu where he lived.

It is, on the other hand, a question of extreme pertinence
to elucidate the relation of the messianic intentions of
Jesus to the eschatological hope of the Old Testament and
of the Jewish people in New Testament times. One could
assume that the role of the Galilean preacher was that of
an epigone or of a reproducer. He said himself that he had
come in order not to destroy, but to fulfill, but what is the
meaning of these words? The connections with the religious
history of Israel are evident, but it becomes clear that the
continuity was not straight or uncomplicated. There has
to be supposed something which perhaps can be most strik-
ingly described as a re-creation, whereby the different
elements in Jewish messianology were taken over—conceptions, terms, symbols, social orders, forms of worship—but
were selected, combined, and transformed in such a way
that the result of this process appears as quite a new unit.
We shall try to sketch briefly the process of re-creation by
means of the notions of selection, combination, and transformation.

It is not difficult to notice a conscious *selection* in the
attitude of Jesus toward the messianic hope of his com-
patriots. Many of the components of the scriptural references to the person of the Messiah or of later Jewish
conceptions about the savior-to-come were eliminated or
accused of being inadequate. Here it is worth mentioning

that Jesus emancipated himself from the purely national and immanent idea of the ideal king. This is evidently the reason why he rejected the open use, when speaking of his own person, of the traditional title of Messiah, the anointed One. On the other hand, we find a markedly selective tendency toward the jungle of speculations which had grown around the more transcendent figure of the savior as it was proper to Palestinian apocalyptics. Certainly Jesus used the title of "Son of man" with regard to himself, certainly he placed his person and his activity in a wide eschatological perspective, but the occurrences of the last days, the whole scheme of events, the details of which were in the mind of the apocalyptists, are only touched upon in his utterances, and that in order to interpret the meaning and the consequences of eschatology. There is nothing in the Gospels of the products of a vivid imagination which is characteristic of Jewish apocalypses. We need only point at the discretion which distinguishes the scene of the last judgment in Matthew 25:31–46. All that is said there has reference to man in an essential way. On the other hand nothing is told about impersonal cosmic events. Thus it is obvious that the messianic terms used by Jesus are to be found in the Old Testament and in later Jewish literature, and there they have, as a matter of course, to be analyzed in their context. The decisive feature, however, lies in the manner in which certain elements have been taken over, while others have been rejected.

Further, the teaching of Jesus about his own nature has received its individual characteristics from the *combination* of traditional elements and ideas. There is a good deal of creative work in the way in which extant data are put together. Three currents of Jewish messianic conceptions have been united or reintegrated in a manner to which there is no analogy in the history of Israelite religion. These currents are the figures of the Messiah (in a narrowed sense of the word), of the Son of man, and of the Ebed Yahweh. Without entering into the question of whether the Son of man in single passages in the apocalyptic literature has been connected with the Servant of the Lord of Deutero-Isaiah, we can establish that the combination of the motifs of victory and suffering characteristic of New Testament Christology, and thus undoubtedly of the teaching of Jesus, is distinguished by its radical and concrete form from all previous messianology. Variations of the same antithetical combination are martyrdom and glory as well as humility and authority.

One of the results of this combination of the ideas of the Messiah and of the Son of man is that we can trace, in the person of Jesus and in his words about himself, the concrete realism of the immanent hope of the Messiah and also something of the transcendence characteristic of the idea of the Son of man. In spite of its supranational breadth which is proper to the gospel of the kingdom of God, the life and activity of Jesus is bound up with and restricted to the Jewish people. The messianic hope of Israel must first be accomplished, and that is the presupposition for the fulfilling of the real aim of Christ's coming: the proclamation of the gospel of salvation to the whole world. Having this goal in view he gathered around him the chosen people, the new Israel, and had already organized it during his lifetime as a real community, a social body, in the midst of this world. In this community, which at the same time represents the new covenant between God and mankind, the blessings of the coming age are given to its members, certainly not yet in their fullness, but anticipated as firstfruits. In the mighty works and miracles performed by Jesus during his ministry—and succeeded later in the church by the sacraments—in the salvation of judgment actualized by

45

the preaching of the gospel, eschatology is already realized, i.e., life released from its limitations is being experienced, changing human beings and their mutual relations. That means that some of the features of the immanent messianic hope are actualized, though bearing a mark of transcendence. On the other hand, the waiting for the second coming of Christ, the belief in cosmic revolutions preceding the appearance of the heavenly savior, in the realization of the age to come by catastrophes annihilating heaven and earth, in the resurrection of the dead, the last judgment, and a new existence—all these elements associated with Christology have their background in the Jewish conceptions of the transcendence of the Son of man, though the sayings of Jesus about these events take into consideration in a much clearer way the relation of eschatology to actual human life.

The third creative process, that of *transformation*, has operated upon all the motifs and elements which in the words and deeds of Jesus have been selected from Jewish eschatology and which, having been combined in a unique way, constitute the picture of Jesus the Christ which emerges from the texts of the New Testament. Here we still presuppose that Jesus himself was the author of this christological conception. Transformation is in reality the essence of the re-creation which in New Testament terminology is called fulfillment. If we take the motif of kingship, we see in what a radical way it has been changed. Christ is really king in the fullest sense of the word, but apart from the nature of his kingdom, his glory is the result not of his power, but of his service. His victory is won not in a fight against nations or cosmic powers, but by obedience and suffering. The priestly function of Christ is performed not in the temple of Jerusalem or in an ideal sanctuary of a similar kind, but in the sacrifice of the cross, interpreted and communicated by the sacrament of the Last Supper. The three functions mentioned, those of the king, the high priest, and the prophet, break all national boundaries without losing their immediate relation to the life of men. The organism of the church as it takes shape after the resurrection is clearly conceived and prefigured, with its specific features, during the ministry of Jesus. And yet both the activity of Jesus and the function of the church point forward to a final consummation.

The most sublime and most essential result of the creative process which has formed Christology is the conception of the mission of Christ in its entirety. The outlines of this conception are to be found in the sayings of Jesus about the Son of man, and there is no need to suspect these sayings of being spurious or to doubt that Jesus identified himself with the Son of man. According to the words of Jesus, the savior is a heavenly being, the Son of God who has assumed humanity, who is to suffer and to die, who will be raised from the dead, exalted to a heavenly dominion, and who will return for a final judgment. The ingredients of this soteriological drama have likewise been preformed in Israelite cult and in later Jewish eschatology, and still there is no equivalent to it within Judaism. In this conception of the mission of Christ, there are of course very distinct transcendental elements which are withdrawn from every attempt at a historical proof of what really happened. The New Testament scholar can only establish that this soteriology, this outline of the mission of Christ, is indissoluble from the gospel of Jesus as a whole. On the other hand, he is obliged to analyze the meaning and the religious message of this kind of Christology including the partly transcendental mission of the Son of man.

The interpretation of the content of the Christology created and taught by Jesus had already been begun in the preaching of the primitive church from its first days. We can trace this work in the witness of the disciples of Jesus referred to in the first chapters of the Acts of the Apostles. Perhaps the main contribution of Paul to Christianity is his evolution of christological thinking. His everlasting merit is to have carried out the translation—which of course had been inaugurated in the Church of Jerusalem from its beginnings—of the gospel of Christ and the gospel about Christ not only into the Greek language, but above all into modes of thought intelligible to the Greek. The title of "Messiah," central in Jewish eschatology, has in its Greek equivalent become a mere proper name, *Christos*. In its place another characterizing epithet appears which is given a specific theological content all over the Hellenistic and Roman world. It is the term *kurios*, "Lord," which certainly renders the Aramaic *maran* or *marana*, but which, because of its suitableness, gained a special importance. The sentence "Jesus Christ is Lord"—or "Our Lord is Jesus Christ"—was fitted to transcend all frontiers and thus made the world mission possible. What is meant by the term "Lord" has to be expounded by preaching and teaching, the basis for which is being laid by theological reflection.

What about the title of "Son of man" in the history of the primitive Church? We find it, apart from the Gospels, only once in Acts (7:56) and twice in Revelation (1:13; 14:14). The reason for this fact seems to be that during the ministry of Jesus the messianic or christological dogma was involved in this name, which from different points of view was fitted to be employed by Jesus. In the situation of the church the term became superfluous. For the mystery of the Son of man had been succeeded by the witness about Jesus Christ, his incarnation, suffering, and resurrection. With a slight exaggeration one could say that the Son-of-man Christology of the Gospels has given place to the preaching and creed of the Christian church. At the same time we notice that there is a solid tradition in the Gospels, in many respects older and more primitive than the theology of the church, at the moment when they were written down. This comes out from the very fact that the primitive mystery of the Son of man has been so clearly preserved in the Gospels.

Thus it is, and it has always been, the task of New Testament exegesis to work out the components of Christology in order to understand and to interpret the intention of Jesus and the meaning of his sayings and actions. But the very essence of these components will appear more clearly in the measure that we are able to elucidate the process of development which they have undergone, in Old Testament times and in later Judaism, before being incorporated in the christological synthesis. The study of the mythological background of the Christology of Jesus and of the primitive church is therefore necessary for a thorough understanding of the gospel itself.

III. On the Composition
of the Gospel of Mark

The literary character and origin of the Gospels, as well as the assumptions we have to reckon with as a background to the source of the Gospels in the form in which they are handed down, belong to the New Testament problems which now, as earlier, engage research even though there has been no success in reaching any generally accepted solution. In the realm of synoptic exegesis the "classical" two document hypothesis, with the Gospel of Mark and the supposed logia source as background to the Gospels of Matthew and Luke, stands in no way unchallenged,[1] and, in any case, the contours and profiles of the hypothetical collection of logia stand out rather indistinctly, even if we must inevitably assume some sort of tradition in material over and above what was set down in the Gospel of Mark. The view which is gaining ground, however, indicates that the simple and schematic solutions are not admissible in the long run. We must come to terms with rather involved connections in the tradition. What further complicates the position of research is that it is not only a question of difficult literary-historical problems, as is the case, for instance, with the Homeric epics. Rather it is inevitable that the innumerable contributions devoted to Gospel research are stamped to a greater or lesser degree by the attitude of the writer in question toward the person and character of Jesus. The fatal thing is that there actually is no such

[1]See, e.g., Basil C. Butler, *The Originality of St. Matthew: A critique of the two-document hypothesis* (London: Cambridge University Press, 1951). L. Vaganay, *Le problème synoptique* (Paris: Tournai, 1954).

thing as research without presuppositions. The more emancipated a scholar thinks he is, the less he is in actual fact.
In the interest of research, however—and in order to get as
far as possible in spite of the problem of presuppositions—
it is a question of being conscious that a fundamental difficulty in every treatment of the Gospels, both as to their
form and their content, lies in the fact that the assumption
behind our Gospels is the gospel of Jesus Christ, which in
turn has its origin and its purpose in the person of Jesus.

This difficulty in reaching an objective analysis and thus
a *consensus* of scholarship—at present we are still far from
such—becomes evident if we keep to the synoptic Gospels,
especially to the Gospel of Mark, since it should appro-
priately be taken as the starting point in an investigation of
the synoptic problems. For however one conceives of the
underlying tradition-history, it is, so to speak, most natural
to begin the unwinding of the synoptic threads at Mark's
end. But it is also necessary that the problems of composition, the questions of the nature and form of the tradition
material and of its remolding by the evangelist, require a
fundamental, and thus even in other connections important,
answer in the first place with regard to the second of
our Gospels.

Where it is a question of the tradition from the time of
the life of Jesus to the fixing of the Gospel of Mark in its
present form—when we must consider that at least during
the latter part of this period an oral and a written tradition
existed side by side—it is inevitable that the basic element
of the tradition material be comprised of separate pericopes
and of groups of such pericopes. On this point, the form-
critical school has made a profitable and a lasting contribution, even if the more far-reaching and valued conclusions
sometimes drawn by the representatives of this line of research have not in the long run retained the same striking

obviousness.[2] It would thus be naïve to imagine that the tradition as such had been formed entirely of independent narrative elements or of sayings of Jesus. We must rather proceed from the fact that to the sum of various pericopes comes a dominating and coordinating factor in the tradition, partly coinciding with what in more recent exegesis is usually termed "kerygma." This, the message about the crucified and risen Christ, must have been the prerequisite and the basis for all Gospel tradition. Within the framework of this kerygma even the mention of the life of Jesus on earth has its given place.[3] For without historical support for the life of Jesus, the tidings of his death and resurrection would lack an essential element. From this it follows that the kerygma and Gospel tradition by their nature and from the very beginning must have been interwoven and dependent on each other, and this in turn compels us to reckon with a factor which has disciplined and controlled the tradition. Its material could not have floated around freely and uncoordinated, nor could it have grown and multiplied entirely in accordance with the whims and fancies of preachers and narrators. In actual fact, a sort of force of gravitation has been found in it which has kept together the elements of tradition and asserted itself both in their content and in their form. That force was quite simply the early church's picture of Jesus, which received its individual character from what had taken place and had been experienced. The vital realization that the Gospels should not be regarded as chronicles simply permitting themselves to be used to present historically the outward course of the life

[2]For references and criticism of the work of the form-critical school see, e.g., Manson, *Jesus the Messiah*, pp. 20 ff.; Alan H. McNeile, *An Introduction to the New Testament* (2nd rev. ed.; New York: Oxford University Press, 1953), pp. 46 ff.; Alfred Wikenhauser, *New Testament Introduction*, trans. Joseph Cunningham (New York: Herder & Herder, 1958), pp. 253 ff. Cf. also Benoit, "Reflexions," pp. 481–512.
[3]See, e.g., Dodd, *Apostolic Preaching*, pp. 21, 48.

of Jesus, nor as travel diaries chronologically describing the course of the wanderings of Jesus, in its turn requires as complement the supposition that the early church's preaching and teaching did not only build on the relatively independent pericopes of the words of Jesus or stories from his life, but also on a complete picture of the person and life of Jesus, which had a firm basis in the belief of the community. This belief, furthermore, was grounded in previous historical events which were experienced and witnessed by people who still lived and acted as tradition bearers at the time when the Gospel tradition—at least the synoptic Gospel tradition—received its final written form. The greater the importance attached to the person of Jesus in respect to the forming of the circle of disciples and the origin of the church, the more reason there is to reckon with the firmness and dominance of the general impression which emanated from his person and the outward course of his life.

From the general construction of the Gospel of Mark, as well as from details in the form, it appears that this Gospel is the work of a man who, with firm grip and with a definite theological view, has arranged and molded the material handed down. It is inevitable that the evangelist found himself in living contact with the preaching and teaching of the church of his time, but he was certainly more than a mere exponent of an anonymous community's views and opinions. Rather he seems to have belonged to the leading figures within early Christendom who had the ability comprehensively to select and systematize the material. Here our intention is not to go more deeply into this theological and literary work of the evangelist, which comes to light in a multitude of characteristic details. Instead we wish to limit ourselves to making in one respect a limited contribution to the illumination of the question of the composition of the

Gospel. The prerequisite for the contribution of the evangelist is tradition: the tradition is the bearer of the material which forms the basis of the description of the life and activity of Jesus. The evangelist's own contribution lies in the editorship, in the forming and arranging of this material. Now it has already been pointed out that we must start from the fact that in the traditional material a connected picture of Jesus has already been found, that is, a complete view of his person and life. Insofar as the evangelist systematizes, he also works with a complete picture which he seeks to express in the contours of his work. The problem then arises: is it conceivable that the evangelist's systematized picture of Jesus in some respects differs from that of the tradition behind it, and is there some possibility of finding such differences in the present form of the Gospel of Mark? In what follows, an attempt will be made to answer this question at some points.

The arrangement of the material in the second Gospel is not easy to understand. This fact becomes clear from a study of the interpretations of this Gospel, which reveal quite different attempts to sort out the material. The story of the passion and the attached short account of the resurrection (chaps. 14–16:8) admittedly form a self-contained element, but in the remainder of the Gospel it is not possible to find starting points for any similarly obvious division. Not even chapters 11–13 form a self-contained unit, because, on the one hand, they are closely connected with the preceding description of the ministry and teaching of Jesus, and, on the other, they prepare and introduce the account of the passion and death of Jesus. This is particularly the case with chapter 13, where the motif from the story of the passion is taken up in an anticipatory way.[4]

---

[4]On this see Robert H. Lightfoot, *The Gospel Message of St. Mark* (New York: Oxford University Press, 1950), pp. 48 ff.

In general terms, we can nevertheless draw the following outlines for Mark's presentation of the life of Jesus up to the beginning of the story of the passion: the baptism and ministry and wanderings in Galilee and surrounding districts (chaps. 1–9), the journey to Jerusalem (chap. 10), the entry and preaching in the capital during the days before the passion (chaps. 11–13). This plan in all its brevity agrees, however, in a striking way with the kerygmatic wording, rooted in the preaching of the early community in Jerusalem, which Dodd has shown in the sermons of the apostles reproduced in Acts.[5] This consistency appears above all in a comparison with the following passage from Peter's speech in Caesarea: "The word which was proclaimed throughout all Judea, beginning from Galilee after the baptism which John preached: how God anointed Jesus of Nazareth with the Holy Spirit and with power; how he went about doing good and healing all that were oppressed by the devil, for God was with him. And we are witnesses to all that he did both in the country of the Jews and in Jerusalem. They put him to death by hanging him on a tree" (Acts 10:37–39). The same basic plan of the outer course of the life of Jesus is again briefly expressed in the following passage: "And for many days he appeared to those who came up with him from Galilee to Jerusalem" (Acts 13:31). It appears to be reasonable to assume that here it is a question of an original and basic feature in the life of Jesus, even if it has been somewhat simplified by being stylized. This description of the development of events, which in the final instance probably goes back to the life itself, has already at an early stage set its stamp on the Gospel tradition as it can be reconstructed with the help of the quoted words from Acts. The consequence of this was that the pericopes with expressly geographical links (e.g., the stories from Capernaum

[5]Dodd, *Apostolic Preaching*, pp. 17 ff.

56

in Mark 1, the acknowledgment of Jesus as Messiah in 8:27 ff., and what is stated about the appearance of Jesus in Jerusalem and its surroundings in chapters 11–13), were from the beginning of the Gospel tradition organized in accordance with these relatively basic passages.[6]

Beside this arrangement, which builds on the real, or rather the stylized, course of the life of Jesus (naturally in association with reality), runs another basic plan in the Gospel of Mark, a plan of systematic or christological type which shows a clear transition between 8:26 and 8:27. After the introduction, which includes John the Baptist's appearance and the baptism of Jesus (1:1–13),[7] follows the first main part, which may be characterized under the heading "the Son of man and Israel,"[8] and which contains the description partly of the ministry of Jesus among the people and partly of the opposition raised against him (1:14–8:26). The other main part, which runs from 8:27 to 13:37, may be said to deal with the subject "the Messiah as teacher and prophet," where the first subdivision, 8:27–10:52, is introduced by Peter's confession at Caesarea Philippi and the transfiguration on the mountain, and then deals with the teaching and education of the disciples by Jesus, who is not only their Master, but also the Messiah of the time of salvation. The other subdivision, 11:1–13:37, begins with the messianic demonstration of the entry into Jerusalem and then passes over to the teaching about authority and perfection. This in turn leads up to the description of the passion and the crucifixion.

This last-named arrangement bears undeniable features of theological, or rather christological, reflection, the origi-

---

[6]On the problem of the reconstruction of the historical course of the ministry of Jesus see Thomas W. Manson, *The Servant-Messiah* (London: Cambridge University Press, 1953), pp. 65 ff., 77 ff.

[7]Concerning this division see Lightfoot, *Gospel Message*, pp. 16 ff.

[8]A. Fridrichsen, *Markusevangeliet* (1952), p. 41.

his predecessors in the chain of tradition. The first of these nator of which could be the evangelist himself or one of alternatives seems to be the more likely. A quick glance at the material shows already at this stage—something which will be confirmed also during the continued course of this investigation—that the historically stylized arrangement is the original, while the christologically systematic is super-imposed, probably as a work of the evangelist. With this statement we arrive at a different result from Cerfaux, who in a recent work on the synoptic question asserts that the systematic arrangement of the Gospel material in the Gospel of Matthew, built upon the teaching of the church, is older than the biographically descriptive presentation in the Gospel of Mark.[9]

It has rightly been pointed out that the gathering together and molding of the material in the first subdivision of the second main part (i.e., 8:27–10:52), has taken place with the situation of the church after Easter and Pentecost in mind. As distinguished from the first part of the Gospel of Mark, where the mighty works of Jesus and his preaching in Galilee stand in the foreground, we are confronted here with teaching directed above all to the circle of disciples to whom an insight is given into what is meant by the way of discipleship and by life in the fellowship where the Messiah is the focal point and the mediator of the demands and possibilities of the coming kingdom of God. In chapters 11–13 the heightened circumstances during the fateful days in Jerusalem before the passion and death admittedly domi-nate, but nevertheless, most of the material in these chapters is of a didactic nature. Even the two messianic demonstra-tions within the second main part, namely the transfigura-tion on the mountain (9:2–8) and the entry into Jerusalem

---

[9]L. Cerfaux, *La mission de Galilee dans la tradition synoptique* (Ana-lecta Lov. Bibl. et Or. 1, Ser. 2:36, 1952), p. 23.

(11:1–11), blend well with the didactic material. In particular, this applies to the transfiguration, where the anticipated revelation of the messianic glory is reserved for the inner circle of disciples.

Naturally, it is not in itself impossible that, during the latter part of his ministry and after experiencing the growing opposition from the side of the people and their leaders, Jesus withdrew from the public eye and instead devoted himself especially to the training of a small group of followers. Such a view of the historical course of events has often been advanced in research into the life of Jesus, above all during the so-called liberal period when it was believed that a psychologically credible picture of the development of Jesus himself could be reconstructed. However, there are signs in the presentation in the Gospel of Mark which indicate that the characteristic concentration of didactic material, mainly intended for the education of the disciples, was not found in the original tradition material but is the result of the evangelist's editorial activity. Thus the picture of Jesus, as first publicly active in Galilee preaching and performing miracles and thereafter limiting his activity more or less to the circle of disciples, is not a primary datum in the tradition, but a secondary event the origin of which may most likely be attributed to the evangelist.[10]

If there really had first been a stage when Jesus publicly appeared in Galilee preaching God's kingdom and doing mighty works, and then a second period had followed when, driven by outward opposition and disappointment, Jesus had limited himself to teaching and educating a limited number of disciples, this development would be found in all traditional material and would appear more or less uniformly in its various parts. Above all—to take an example

[10]The systematizing of the tradition material in Mark has been dealt with by Lightfoot, *Gospel Message*, pp. 31–47.

from a detail not unessential in this connection—the occurrence of the term διδάσκω and words derived therefrom should in this case be determined by the change which occurred in the way in which Jesus came and ministered, so that the group of words in question should be reserved for the stories from the later part of the ministry of Jesus. Thus διδάσκω and related words should be found mainly in the passage Mark 8:27–13:37. However, this is in no way the case. Already in the first chapter of Mark, and thereafter in several places, in the description of the appearance of Jesus in Galilee and neighboring parts, it is said that Jesus taught, and that he did this "with power." In the synagogues and before the people he appeared as teacher, and this side of the ministry of Jesus is not the same as the preaching of the kingdom of God.[11] In actual fact, there is a difference between διδάσκω and κηρύσσω, even if these two forms of activity appear side by side during the wanderings of Jesus in Galilee.[12] That teaching was understood as a characteristic feature in the ministry of Jesus is apparent from the fact that Jesus was called teacher (διδάσκαλος ῥαββί) not only by his closest disciples,[13] but also by those more on the fringe.[14] That teaching was considered to be an essential part of the messianic task of Jesus is expressed also in the detail that, at the sending out of the disciples into Galilee, teaching is mentioned as a complement to the mighty works which they were called upon to perform. When they returned from their missionary journeys "[they] told him all that they had done and taught" (Mark 6:30). In this connection it should be noted that the sending out of the disciples on the one hand means an anticipation of the mission after Easter

[11] Mark 1:21, 22; 2:13; 4:1, 2; 6:2, 6, 34; Mark 1:22, 27; 4:2.
[12] In Mark the terms διδάσκω and κηρύσσω do not appear in the vicinity of each other.
[13] Mark 4:38 and other places.
[14] Mark 5:35; 10:17.

and Pentecost, and, on the other hand, it mirrors the ministry of Jesus himself: the disciples "represent" their master by letting the presence of the kingdom of God take expression in the same mighty works, the same message, and the same teaching as was the case with Jesus.[15] When the disciples' preliminary mission coincides with the time of the public ministry of Jesus in Galilee, when we can see in the Gospel accounts of it a reflection of the ministry of Jesus himself in the same Palestinian milieu, and when the teaching is expressly attached to the activity of the disciples during the same period, this means that the picture of the coming of Jesus as teacher among the people of Galilee is further corroborated.

What is now implied by the fact that Jesus not only preached but also taught? On this point Mark in the first part of his Gospel is rather silent. He mentions the teaching of Jesus but does not recount much of its content. In this he differs in a striking way from both Matthew and Luke, who both allow the didactic material from the tradition to be represented at the very beginning of the description of the coming of Jesus, as for example in the Sermon on the Mount in the first Gospel (Matt. 5–7). Only in one passage in the first part of the Gospel of Mark are we faced with the meaning of what Jesus taught, and that is in the sequence of parables about the kingdom of heaven: the sower, the lamp under a bushel, the seed which grew by itself, and the grain of mustard seed (Mark 4:1–34). In the introduction to this collection of parables, it is expressly stated that it is a question of teaching: "Again he began to teach beside the sea. . . . And he taught them many things in parables" (Mark 4:1 f.). This sort of teaching thus seems

---

[15]Cf. the writer's investigation, "Ämbetet i Nya Testamentet," in *En bok om kyrkans ämbete* (Stockholm: 1951).

to be indissolubly bound up with the picture of the Galilean ministry of Jesus.

By way of distinction from this, we may observe that the second part of the Gospel of Mark, that is 8:27—13:37, leaves a much fuller picture of the content of the didactic statements of Jesus. Already in purely external respects this appears in the fact that the verb διδάσκω and the noun διδαχή, where they occur, are syntactically connected with closer definition. It may be a question of an accusative object: "but truly teach the way of God" (12:14), or an affirmative sentence introduced by the word διδάσκειν: "And he began to teach them that the Son of man must suffer many things" (8:31; cf. 9:31). In other contexts also the words of Jesus are introduced by a statement that it is a question of teaching so far as Jesus was concerned: "And he taught, and said to them . . ." (11:17; cf. 12:35, 38). A general saying about his teaching activity, ". . . and crowds gathered to him again; and again, as his custom was, he taught them" (10:1), forms the introduction to the collection of didactic material in chapter 10. One general reference, not closely defined, to the content of the teaching ministry of Jesus occurs in the second part of the Gospel, and this in a brief statement about the determination of the Jewish leaders to put Jesus to death. As a motive for this is given their fear of the effects of his teaching (11:18; cf. 14:49).

Before we draw any conclusions from the observations so far made concerning the Gospel of Mark, it may be appropriate to look briefly at the two verbs διδάσκω and κηρύσσω and the conception they represent in the account of the evangelist Mark.[16] That they are not equivalents, but

---

[16]On this see also H. Odeberg, " 'Lära' i Nya Testamentet," *Erevna*, 9 (1952): 80–83; "Urkristen lära och undervisning," *ibid.*, pp. 91–99. Cf. also E. Fascher, "Jesus der Lehrer," *Theol. Literaturztg.*, vol. 79 (1954), cols. 325–42.

represent different sides of what Jesus uttered has already been stated. The difference stands out most clearly on glancing at the objects which are connected with the verb κηρύσσω. Thus it is said that John the Baptist preached "a baptism of repentance for the forgiveness of sins" (1:4), that Jesus preached "the gospel of God," which meant that "the time is fulfilled, and the kingdom of God is at hand" (1:14; cf. 13:10). The disciples went out on their missionary errands with the challenging proclamation for the people "that men should repent" (6:12). And when such as had been healed by Jesus in their turn "proclaimed" what had befallen them, this means that they acknowledged the fundamental fact of salvation which they had experienced (1:45; 5:20; 7:36). Another characteristic feature lies in the fact that the activity designated by κηρύσσω is directly and expressly represented as comparable with the mighty works and miracles: "And he went throughout all Galilee, preaching in their synagogues and casting out demons" (1:39); "and he appointed twelve, to be with him, and to be sent out to preach and have authority to cast out demons" (3:14 f.). About the disciples we further read: "So they went out and preached that men should repent. And they cast out many demons, and anointed with oil many that were sick and healed them" (6:12 f.). It is clear that the evangelist by the verb κηρύσσω denotes the propounding of the fundamental message of salvation: the necessity to repent and the proclamation of the immediate coming of the kingdom of God. It has rightly been asserted as a sign of the special Christology of the Gospel of Mark that the proclamation by Jesus of the kingdom of God and his mighty works give expression in two different ways to one and the same thing: in words the presence of the kingdom of God is proclaimed, and in miracles it takes shape among men and demonstrates its power.[17] Therefore it is not by chance that the kerygma of Jesus and his mighty works are terminologically on a par and connected with each other in the way shown above. In distinction from the proclamation of the kerygma, the awakening and comforting message, "the news" about the kingdom of God, the teaching, διδαχή, aims at leading deeper into its nature and its now-revealed secret to those who have come to listen and who have been won over by the message. "To you has been given the μυστήριον of the kingdom of God"—so we read in the didactic chapter in the former part of the Gospel of Mark (Mark 4:11). Through teaching, understanding[18] and education are given, and this means that the teaching complements the kerygmatic proclamation (and the mighty works) and chronologically follows them.

What can we now conclude from the observations which have been made regarding the occurrence of διδάσκω in the Gospel of Mark? Without doubt the ministry of Jesus as teacher is firmly anchored in the tradition lying behind the Gospel, as is also the case with the other synoptic traditions in their various branches. Furthermore, it may be noted, and here the Gospel of Mark agrees also with the other Gospels, that Jesus stood out as a teacher during the whole time of his public ministry, that is, in Galilee as well as during the wanderings to and through Judea and afterwards, even during the days before the trial in Jerusalem. Jesus was not only a prophet in the proclamative meaning. He not only confronted men with the tidings of God's kingdom, but he was also a teacher, in that, starting with his people's old traditions of teaching, he spoke, interpreted,

---

[17]This has been shown in an illuminating way above all by W. Manson, *Jesus the Messiah*, pp. 32–50.

[18]The term γνῶσις is used mainly by Paul, but in Mark the verb γινώσκειν is used in a meaning which is of interest in this context (4:13; 12:12; 13:28 f.). This meaning is common above all in the Fourth Gospel.

and gave instruction in the synagogues of Galilee, out in the open air, among a circle of listeners, followers, and disciples, or in the precincts of the temple in Jerusalem.[19]

The evangelist's efforts to systematize the adopted material diverges, however, from this picture which clearly belongs to a tradition which is older than the Gospel in its present form. Here it seems possible to gain an insight into the editorial elements in the Gospel and thus into the evangelist's method of proceeding. While the earlier tradition, still preserved in the summarizing descriptions of the ministry of Jesus (e.g., "And they went into Capernaum; and immediately on the sabbath he entered the synagogue and taught. And they were astonished at his teaching," Mark 1:21 f.), permits the preaching and teaching of Jesus (from the appearance in Galilee to the last days in the capital) to appear parallel, the evangelist seeks to divide the material into two parts. The effect is that he concentrates the kerygmatic side of Jesus' ministry (including the accounts of the miracles) in the first part of his writings, while in the second part of his Gospel he groups together the traditions about the teaching of Jesus. As has been pointed out, the exception is the parables about the kingdom of God, which belong so closely to the actual kerygmatic message that they are not easily distinguished from it. The result of the division made by the evangelist is that to the former part of Mark's writing (1:14–8:26) we can put the heading "call," while the latter part (8:27–13:37, though from 11:1 other material also comes in) may be collected under the heading "discipleship." What is the reason for such a systematizing of the material? Without doubt it was necessitated by the church's position at the time of the editing of the material. As Christian teaching had been systematized and consolidated during the first decades of

[19] Cf. K. H. Rengstorf, διδάσκω, in Kittel, vol. 2.

the early church, something we know thanks to the New Testament epistles, it was felt suitable to bring together the teaching material in the tradition about Jesus to show that "the doctrine" of the Christian life had its origin in the actual teaching of Jesus. The disciples thus become prototypes for Christians who are led into the way of discipleship. The division of the description of the ministry of Jesus into two parts in actual fact has its equivalent in the twofold nature of the missionary message and sermon in the activity of the early church. The early Christian missionary message was also the "kerygmatic" one in that its essence was the message about Jesus Christ, his earthly life, passion, death, and resurrection. This is substantiated by all the evidence from the speeches in Acts, the origin of which, as far as the basic plan is concerned, has often been noted in recent times.[20] Now it is admitted that the kerygma of God's kingdom proclaimed by Jesus and the Christ kerygma of the early church differ chiefly in that the latter assumes the events of Easter as historical fact,[21] and this makes the former part of Mark's Gospel and the early Christian missionary message, seen only schematically or in principle, correspond to each other. It is, however, quite another matter with the part dealing with discipleship in Mark and the teaching of the early church. Here there are striking similarities, and there is reason to hold that the evangelist has been influenced by the church position he was in when selecting and forming the traditional material. Naturally such a supposition does not mean that the material handed down in the Gospel should be secondary in relation to Jesus, that is, should have been

[20]In this connection the work of C. H. Dodd has been revolutionary (see p. 8, n. 3, above). Concerning the missionary message and teaching, see also Krister Stendahl, *The School of St. Matthew* (2nd ed.; Philadelphia: Fortress Press, 1968), pp. 13 ff.
[21]The real connecting link between the two kerygmas is formed by the various sayings of Jesus about the Son of man.

66

created by the evangelist or by the traditionalists standing behind him, but it is inevitable—as will also shortly be shown—that the forming of the handed-down pericopes reflects in certain details the situation [*Sitz im Leben*] in which they were told and applied in Christian teaching at the time of their final formulation in connection with the editing of the Gospel.

That the episode at Caesarea Philippi, with Peter's confession on behalf of the disciples (Mark 8:27–29), has formed an important point in the development of the relationship between Jesus and the Twelve who most closely followed him, seems to be inevitable.[22] As the account is placed in Mark, however, it has more than the task of conveying an event, important in itself, occurring during the wanderings of Jesus with his disciples. Rather, the pericope also forms the introduction to the whole of the passage in Mark which contains the didactic material, and this fact permits us to understand that the evangelist-editor has understood the disciples' confession of Jesus as Messiah as the gateway leading into true discipleship, the path of teaching and imitation. The confession of faith here becomes the prerequisite for Jesus to disclose all of his teachings, not only about the deepest purpose of the Son of man, his passion, death, and resurrection, but also about the elemental signs of the disciples' life in the presence of the Master and within the range of the power of the kingdom of God. Thinking of the historical course of events, it is naturally an anomaly that the missionary task of the twelve disciples in Galilee and their teaching in connection therewith occurs prior to what Jesus teaches about the fundamental things of the new life. On the other hand, it is quite the contrary if we think about the position of the

---

[22]This historical question is dealt with by T. W. Manson, *Servant-Messiah*, pp. 71 f., and in *Journal of Theological Studies* N.S. 2 (1952): 201.

church after Easter and Pentecost. There the kerygmatic call leads to confession of faith and baptism, after which teaching within the framework of the community may begin. The accounts of baptism in Acts gives us this picture in general.[23] Thus in the systematizing of Mark's Gospel, the words of Peter, σὺ εἶ ὁ χριστός (8:29), are seen to correspond to the confession of Jesus in the baptism of the early church which formed the origin of discipleship and imitation. It is surely no chance that the term χριστός, which was the church's epithet for "savior," besides occurring in the opening of the Gospel of Mark (1:1) appears first in the Caesarea Philippi pericope and then recurs several times.[24] From that moment, when Peter confessed Jesus as Messiah, the disciples according to Mark find themselves in an anticipatory way in the church's position. Significant in this context is the expression ὅτι χριστοῦ ἐστε in the saying about the reward for those who give the disciples a cup of water to drink because they belong to the Messiah (9:41): here it is the church's terminology which shows through, and this because the statement itself has the same actuality in the situation of the church as in the teaching of Jesus.

Without making the didactic chapters in Mark into an object of more detailed analysis, we shall here only stress that in them we find the same characteristic connection between Christology and ethical teaching (parenesis) as in the early Christian literature in general. The starting point for the teaching about imitation is the words about the passion, death, and resurrection of the Son of man (8:31). The two repetitions of this prophecy (9:31; 10:32 f.) are also like pillars supporting the contents of chapters 9–10. Further, as a conclusion to the actual teaching about

---

[23]Cf. in this connection esp. Rev. 8:37; and see also Oscar Cullmann, *Earliest Christian Confessions*, trans. J. K. S. Reid (2nd ed.; London: Lutterworth Press, 1949).

[24]Therefore χριστός in Mark 1:34 (BW Θ *et al.*) is not original.

discipleship, comes the saying about the serving Son of man (10:45), after the motif of the passion has been varied by the symbolic saying about the baptism and the cup (10:38 f.). From the New Testament epistolary literature may here be given as an example the well-known saying of Paul in Philippians 2:5: "Have this mind among yourselves, which you have in Christ Jesus, who, though he was in the form of God . . . ," along with the domestic code in Ephesians 5:22–6:9, where Christology and ethics are woven into one another in a way very characteristic of early Christian thought. In Mark 11–12 didactic material is mixed both with the fateful events during the course of the few days in Jerusalem and with the prophetically demonstrative appearance of Jesus during this time. Chapter 13 forms a unit of a more isolated nature, containing the eschatological teaching of Jesus with partially apocalyptic features. That this chapter does not in its entirety form a later insertion, but that we here have to do with one side of the didactic presentation of Jesus, is an opinion which now once again is gaining ground.[25] In the evangelist's editing, this passage stands not only as the conclusion to the didactic part, but in an anticipatory and suggestive way takes up the motif which then comes out in the story of the passion.[26] At the same time there also exist here connections between the teaching of Jesus and the doctrine of the church on "the last things."

Even in the didactic part of Mark certain deviations from the plan otherwise carried out by the editor occur—preaching to the people, teaching and the education of the disciples—and just these discrepancies permit us to get an insight into the form of the tradition before the evangelist's editing. Here it is a matter of brief explanations given in

---

[25]On this see Beasley-Murray, *Jesus and the Future.*
[26]See p. 55, n. 4, above.

the various introductions to the pericopes concerning the hearers of the teaching of Jesus. Had the evangelist carried through his plan consistently in every detail, there should only have been the disciples to hear the sayings of Jesus; perhaps one could also think of a slightly wider circle of followers. What were the actual facts? In certain sayings, Jesus very rightly addresses his disciples, by which the Twelve are meant. This is the case with the prophecies of the passion (8:31; 9:31; 10:32) and with the sayings about humility and the spirit of service in their relationship to each other (9:33; 10:41). At times the disciples are brought face to face with their people (9:28), and on certain occasions it is only a lesser number from the circle of the Twelve who are informed of the revelation or the teaching, as in the case of the transfiguration (9:2) and the apocalyptic discourse (13:3; cf. 10:35). In other connections it is said that Jesus in his teaching addresses himself to the masses (ὁ ὄχλος), and this even in such cases where the message refers directly to discipleship and its meaning, as in the words about the bearing of the cross (8:34). It is absolutely inescapable that large parts of the material gathered together in Mark 8:27—10:52 originate from the didactic expositions on the part of Jesus, not in a limited circle of disciples, but before a larger and entirely open circle of hearers (e.g., 10:1, 17, 46).

The first conclusion which may now be drawn from these observations relates to the evangelist, as mentioned above. It is clearly he who has edited the traditional material in such a way that the teaching of Jesus has been collected into an account which may be called "the education of the disciples," with the confession of Peter at Caesarea Philippi as the starting point and presupposition. The reason for this is in all probability that the evangelist wanted to form the tradition about Jesus in such a way that it should

70

become a model, even from a formal point of view, for the teaching of the church at the time of the editing. The other conclusion refers to the actual coming of Jesus. The details in the second part of the Gospel of Mark, like other details in the first part, bear witness that in the original tradition of the ministry of Jesus there was no division between a first phase with kerygmatic preaching about the kingdom of God and a second phase of esoteric teaching for a closer circle of disciples. Rather the preaching and teaching from the beginning of the coming of Jesus ran parallel with each other and complemented each other. The object of the teaching was both the disciples and "the people." A modification must, however, be made on the basis of the texts: the anticipatory interpretations of the Son of man's mission of suffering, death, and resurrection, as well as the anticipatory revelation of his glory (δόξα) at the transfiguration, have been reserved for a smaller, specifically chosen group, partly the Twelve, partly only three of these. Further, a third conclusion may be drawn, and this affects our knowledge of the actual handing down of the Gospel material. The new ground covered during the past decades by the form-critical study of the Gospels means that we have an increased knowledge of the tradition-history of the individual pericopes and the laws which underlie it. A number of problems connected with this, however, do not yet seem to have been finally solved. Thus ever since K. L. Schmidt's pioneering form-historical work[27] it has been looked upon as established fact that "the framework" of a separate traditional element, chiefly, that is, the introductory particulars about time, place, and circumstances, is to be considered the creation of the evangelist, the "cement" by means of which he has united the various pericopes in

[27]K. L. Schmidt, *Der Rahmen der Geschichte Jesu* (Berlin, 1919).

the order he wants to give them. Our examination of the didactic material in Mark has, however, shown that the characteristic feature of certain particulars of the framework is that they do not fit into the evangelist's scheme of composition. This means nothing less than that we have to reckon with the fact that even the details of the framework in certain cases belong to the actual traditional material, and this, thanks to the testimony of those details, shows that that material has greater differentiation and firmness than we have often wanted to recognize.

The observations so far made—on the one hand, the attempt of the editor to give a systematic grouping of the material and, on the other, the relative firmness of the material even in respect to the framework and the information about the circumstances belonging to it—may further be illuminated and confirmed from another side. As earlier shown, the accounts of the miracles are chiefly found in the first part of the Gospel of Mark, and this because they belong to the kerygmatic preaching of Jesus and form an essential part of this side of the ministry of Jesus. How does it then come about that Mark puts in accounts of miracles also in the later, didactic part of his Gospel? Does this not mean that the systematizing presumed by us does not agree with what stands in the text? On a closer examination of the pericopes dealing with the miracles in question— the healing of the boy possessed by an unclean spirit (9:14–29), the cure of blind Bartimaeus (10:46–52), and finally the cursing of the fig tree (11:12–14, 20–25)—we find the answer. As the story of the epileptic boy is presented, it has the form of an apothegm, that is, an episode which terminates in a saying of Jesus. The point is, therefore, not the miracle itself or the confession of faith made by the father of the sick boy, but rather the attitude of Jesus to the problem of the disciples' incapacity to perform mighty works. At any rate this is how Mark has understood the account as he partly stresses in 9:19: "O faithless generation . . . ," and again in 9:29: "This kind cannot be driven out by anything but prayer." In this case the miracle forms only the starting point for the teaching of Jesus about an essential side of discipleship, and this means that the position of the pericope in the teaching material is fully justified. The account of the withering of the fig tree again belongs organically to the prophetic-messianic demonstrations in chapter 11, which take place during the decisive days before the trial. So here occur the entry into Jerusalem (11:1–10) and the purification of the temple (11:15–19), to which the cursing of the fig tree closely belongs from the point of view of content. Mark has also understood the matter in this way, since he has woven together the story of the fig tree and that of the purification of the temple. In both cases it is a matter of symbolic deeds with messianic meaning. When the fig tree, which is a form of "tree of life," does not bear fruit at the coming of the Messiah, it is mercilessly struck by the judgment. Finally, in respect to the pericope about the healing of blind Bartimaeus, from a formal point of view it is a straightforward account of a miracle with no obvious saying of Jesus apart from what belongs to the actual description of the miracle. How can this account justify its place in the collection of didactic material, if such exists? In all likelihood, the reason is to be found in the local nature of the event. In the tradition, the story of blind Bartimaeus has clearly been so firmly connected with Jericho that Mark has not been able to disregard this fact. Therefore, in this case it has become necessary for him to allow the systematic division to be broken by the geographic plan: the Jericho story could not be inserted in the material localized in Galilee and surrounding districts in the first part of the Gospel, but must have its place immediately before the description of the entry into Jerusalem. In this way, it has been also possible to place it just in the transition between the actual didactic material in chapters 9 and 10 and the material belonging to the visit to Jerusalem in chapters 11–13. Thus we have again been able to establish a concession on the part of the evangelist to the tradition he has built on, which in its turn is a witness to the firmness of the tradition—in this case even with regard to a geographical detail, a single place name.

Thus to some degree the fact asserted at the beginning of this investigation has been confirmed, namely, that in what concerns the Gospel of Mark—and this naturally also applies to the other Gospels according to the circumstances—we must reckon with two principles of composition: first, the firm elements of tradition, to which belong both a stylized basic plan of the outward course of the public ministry of Jesus and characteristic details in the "framework" of the pericopes; and secondly, the evangelist's intention from a theological point of view to edit and systematize the material handed down. These two principles cannot simply be united or superimposed on one another. The analysis of the Marcan material has shown rather that here and there the one or other principle falls short, which is the cause of inconsistencies in one direction or another. From the point of view of the exegete the inconsistency is to be seen exclusively as an advantage, for it is this which makes it possible to get a more plastic picture, both of the evangelist's way of working and of the nature of the tradition lying behind him. Thus we also actually come to the complicated and inexhaustible fundamental problem of Gospel research: the relation between the historic event and the respective theological or christological interpretation of this event.

IV. The Messianic Character of the Temptation in the Wilderness

It is no mere coincidence that the Gospel account of the temptation of Christ in the wilderness has given rise to profound research in recent years.[1] Indeed, to the actual extent to which interest has been shown in the complex problem of the Christology of the Gospels—starting from points which are different and sometimes new—it has been possible to establish that the temptation in the wilderness played an important part in the accounts of the events which have been collected to set forth the inauguration of the public ministry of Christ. This is at least the case in the synoptic Gospels, the idea of temptation being absent from the first chapters of the Fourth Gospel.

In a substantial contribution which appeared in 1957, Dom Jacques Dupont has demonstrated that the account of the temptation, Gospels of Mark and Luke, reveals deep theological thought and strict stylization.[2] The kernel of the account seems to go back to the teaching of Jesus to his disciples during the period of his ministry which followed the confession of Peter at Caesarea Philippi. For the fact that the idea of temptation is also to be found elsewhere in the words of Jesus makes likely the hypothesis that he had spoken of temptations which challenged the very nature

[1]See the works indicated by B. M. F. van Iersel, "Der Sohn in den synoptischen Jesusworten. Christusbezeichnung der Gemeinde oder Selbstbezeichnung Jesu?" (*Novum Testamentum,* Supplement, 3) (Leyden, 1961); pp. 165 f.

[2]Jacques Dupont, "L'arrière-fond biblique du récit des Tentations de Jésus," *New Testament Studies* (1956–57), 3: 287–304. Cf. G. H. P. Thompson, "Called-Proved-Obedient. A Study in the Baptism and Temptation Narratives of Matthew and Luke," *Journal of Theological Studies* N.S. 11 (1960): 1–12.

of his mission. The triple scene in our existing Gospels of Matthew and Luke has been formed on an analogy with the temptations of the people of Israel during their wanderings in the wilderness. It is evident that the description of these temptations as it is given in Deuteronomy has also served as a model. The typology which dominates the Gospel story has been elucidated in a convincing way by Dupont, whose analysis we take as our starting point.

If we accept the conclusion that the text in question in Matthew and Luke shows an elaborate typology, presenting the temptations of Christ in the manner of those of the people of Israel, the result is that it is no longer possible to restrict the interpretation of the Gospel account solely to the plane of the psychology of Jesus. The church fathers, it is true, when commenting on this account concentrated their attention on the human nature of Christ, and they consequently stressed the psychological and individual aspects of the various temptations. But this procedure presupposes authenticity, down to the last detail of the three scenes and their dialogues, and literal interpretation. If, on the other hand, the composition is due to a typological conception, this then witnesses to the theological thought of the church. It then becomes clear that in the thought of the early church the temptations have a messianic significance. For he who has been tempted in the manner of the people of Israel in his own person must be the eschatological counterpart of the chosen people, that is to say, the Messiah. This means that the temptations are placed on the level of the history of salvation, with the rejection of the tempter not solely due to the moral force and psychic integrity of Jesus. For just as the behavior of Israel during the wanderings in the wilderness was a picture typical for the whole of its history, so the firmness of Christ was to have consequences for his mission and for all those to whom he spoke.

How can the meaning of the rejection of the devil by Christ be defined more precisely? If theological thought has elaborated the typological structure of the account, it should be possible to analyze its different aspects. The relevant fundamental feature of the typology we have just mentioned is that Christ is manifested as preserving intact his obedience to God. Whereas Israel had tempted God in the desert and had been revealed as disobedient, Christ had remained faithful. So it is he that represents the true Israel.

When the church fathers in their interpretations of the account of the temptation contrast the perfect fidelity of Christ with the fall of the first man, it is also the idea of obedience which they stress, though they throw into relief the psychology of Christ which they contrast with that of Adam.[3] If this exegesis in particular brings out the individual aspect of the attitude of Jesus, it nevertheless takes account of the prefigurative and representative significance of his behavior. The typology of Adam is scarcely in mind, however, in the Gospel accounts of the temptation, although it is possible that the motif of the restoration of paradise was indicated by the wild beasts spoken of in Mark's account.[4]

In underlining the role played by the conception of obedience in the accounts of the temptation, we should mention the affinity which may be noted in the Gospels between the title "Son of God" and the understanding Jesus had of it insofar as he obeyed his heavenly Father.

---

[3]See K. P. Köppen, *Die Auslegung der Versuchungsgeschichte unter besonderer Berücksichtigung der Alten Kirche* (Tübingen, 1961).

[4]A. Feuillet, "L'épisode de la tentation d'après l'évangile selon saint Marc" (1, 12–13), *Estud. Bibl.* 19 (1960): 49–73.

This title "Son of God" is never openly claimed by Jesus himself, but it is evident from a number of his sayings, without doubt authentic, that he was conscious of being the Son of his Father in a very special sense. Thus there exists a connection between the veiled allusions of Jesus and the developed Christology of the church. Consequently, it is legitimate to ask if the combination of "motifs" inspired by the conception that the Son is obedient goes back in substance to the teaching of Jesus. It is evident that the christological thought of the church has applied to the person of Christ the typology, drawn from the Old Testament, that Israel as "son of God" ought to give proof of obedience.[5]

At the time of the composition of the Epistle to the Hebrews, the church had conceived the idea of the obedience of Christ as Son with the help of a previously determined typology: "In the days of his flesh . . . although he was a Son, he learned obedience through what he suffered" (Heb. 5:7 f.). It was only through perfect obedience that he could become "the source of eternal salvation to all who obey him" (5:9). Also in the second chapter of the same epistle, the obedience of Christ forms a central subject, and at the same time the conception of the Son appears. In a context describing Christ as the only Son are the words: "Therefore he had to be made like his brethren in every respect" (2:17). What the verb ὀφείλειν expresses in this sentence is the duty of the Son to perfect the will of the Father, an idea which dominates the exposition of the whole chapter. A variation of the theme occurs in the following passage: "Now Moses was faithful in all God's house as a servant, . . . but Christ was faithful over God's house as a son" (3:5 f.).

[5]Reginald H. Fuller, *The Mission and Achievement of Jesus* (London: SCM Press, 1954), pp. 80–86; B. M. F. van Iersel, "Der Sohn. . . ."

It is a characteristic feature of the Christology of the synoptic Gospels that the title "Son of God" recurs, apart from the account of the temptation, in the accounts of the baptism and the transfiguration, of which the central theme is the mission of Christ conceived as the achievement of the will of God. Insofar as the title "Son of man" expresses the mission of Christ toward his brother men—"For the Son of man also came not to be served but to serve, and to give his life as a ransom for many" (Mark 10:45)— the idea of "Son of God" places the saving work of Christ in the perspective of the history of salvation and sees it from the angle of the will of God.

Finally, to answer the question whether Jesus himself combined the conception of Son with that of obedience, we may draw attention to indications authorizing an affirmative reply. Without entering into a detailed study, we may be satisfied by referring to the prayer in Gethsemane: "Abba, Father, . . . not what I will, but what thou wilt" (Mark 14:36 and parallels) and to its relationship to the Lord's Prayer (Matt. 6:9 ff. and parallel). Further, the christological hymn of the Epistle to the Philippians (Phil. 2:6–8) witnesses in favor of a formation of the conception of the obedience of Christ as Son, which seems to be independent of the typology revealed in the Epistle to the Hebrews. It is likewise against the background of this obedience that it is necessary to explain the fact that the synoptic tradition describes the unclean spirits as calling Jesus, in a very characteristic manner, "Son of God" (Mark 3:11; Luke 4:41; Mark 5:17; Matt. 8:29; Luke 8:28; cf. Mark 1:24 and Luke 4:34). From this point of view we may compare the accounts of the unclean spirits with that of the temptation. It is indeed evident that the title "Son of God," which recurs in the exclamations of the unclean spirits, has as its object the expression of the fact that the power of Jesus to bind and cast out unclean spirits (Mark 3:23–27) depends on the fact that he is obedient and thereby the "Holy One of God" (Mark 1:24 and Luke 4:34). From then on neither Satan nor the unclean spirits can have power over him, and their domination is thus destroyed.

If the account of the temptation in its three synoptic forms has been doubtlessly placed deliberately at the beginning of the public ministry of Jesus and immediately after the account of the baptism, this may be due to a typological uniting of the baptism and the temptation on the basis of the account of the passage through the Red Sea and of the journey through the wilderness. But further, as proof of Jesus' obedience, the account of the temptation has an organic position between the account of the baptism as the inauguration of the messianic task and that of the public ministry as the realization of the will of God. We wonder, however, whether the rich symbolism of the scenes which enter into the accounts of the temptation in Matthew and Luke has not become an occasion to define the ideas which had been formed about the obedience of the "Son of God."

For the exegesis of the New Testament texts, scholars have been able to derive much profit from a profound analysis of the symbols, metaphors, and pictures which are at the basis of expressions, parables, and whole scenes. This is true especially of the Gospels which offer a wealth of figurative expressions. It is evident that the characteristic features of this language go back to Jesus, whose manner of expression has been preserved by the Gospel tradition. The eloquence and pedagogy of his language consist in the pictures and metaphors not only having been drawn from daily life in Palestine, but in having originated—not all, but the most important of them—from the Old Testament and in having their own place in the religious tradition of the Jewish people. The listeners to whom Jesus addressed himself—both those who followed him and those who rejected him—had all been brought up in this tradition and were thus familiar with this parabolic language in all its richness.[6]

The symbolic and metaphorical language of the Gospels— and it must be remembered that not only the words of Jesus, but also his deeds were charged with a symbolic meaning—has an extremely complicated and profound structure, because it is filled with such associations. These go back, on the one hand, to the Old Testament and consequently actualize a fund of memories, ideas, feelings, and hopes which form an indispensable background to the Good News. On the other hand, the associations extend, so to speak, horizontally, that is to say, through the preaching of Jesus and the texts of the Gospels. It is obvious that already in the words and deeds of Jesus there are intentional connections established by the interpreter of symbolic pictures. Let us refer to pictures such as the sowing and the harvesting or the building upon a rock. These associations of a metaphorical nature help to reunite the various elements of the teaching and ministry of Jesus in a way which the explicit references cannot attain.

Let us take as an example the picture of the shepherd and the sheep. When Jesus uttered the parable of the lost sheep he did not, in the first place, describe an incident of everyday life. It is thus, as we know, that A. Jülicher, the pioneer of the interpretation of the parables in modern times, has wished to explain most of them, starting from suppositions which are too restrained or too rationalistic. On the contrary, as we have urged elsewhere,[7] the shepherd

---

[6]Ian T. Ramsey, *Religious Language* (New York: Macmillan, 1963).
[7]See p. 151 below.

in the parable behaves in a manner quite contrary to the rules of prudence and experience when he leaves his flock to go in search of the one lost sheep. On the other hand, the parable takes its meaning from the fact that it is marked by associations with texts such as Psalm 23: "The LORD is my Shepherd, I shall not want," and especially with the well-known chapter from the book of Ezekiel, where the good shepherd is contrasted with the bad shepherds: "For thus says the Lord GOD: Behold, I, I myself will search for my sheep. . . . As a shepherd seeks out his flock when some of his sheep have been scattered abroad, so will I seek out my sheep; and I will rescue them from all places where they have been scattered on a day of clouds and thick darkness" (Ezek. 34:11 f.). This is one example taken from the many contributions which the Old Testament gives to the deep meaning of the parables. But this parable, as several commentators have stressed, is Christocentric in an indirect way. This means that it does not express a common truth or a permanent idea. Furthermore, the parable in its concrete form proclaims—or hints at—the event which is in process of being realized around Christ who had pity on the crowd "because they were like sheep without a shepherd" (Mark 6:34). In characterizing Christ in this way, the evangelist has expressly identified Jesus, as he announces the coming of the kingdom of God, with the good shepherd of the parable, an identification which already underlies the parable itself.

The biblical symbols are, however, still more complicated. The good shepherd, as distinct from everything practiced in ordinary life, is also he who gives his life for his sheep (John 10:11). The picture of the shepherd occurs again, moreover, in the picture of the last judgment, where the Son of man coming in his glory separates the sheep from the goats in his capacity of shepherd (Matt. 25:31 f.). In following the applications of the same symbolism, we come to the passage where the apostles receive the mission to act as shepherds of the sheep (e.g., John 21:15–17; cf. 1 Pet. 5:2–4).

Here we are faced with a phenomenon characteristic not only of the Gospels or of the whole Bible, but of common religious language. An analysis of poetic language moreover gives similar evidence. It is thanks to the "multivalence of symbols"—a phenomenon which has been studied in several modern works—that various sayings are collected together in a unity of complex ideas, not by explicit statements, but with the help of underlying associations. Thus the picture of the shepherd and sheep, which occurs again in numerous New Testament passages, gathers into a whole the ideas of the coming of the kingdom of God, of divine mercy, salvation, judgment, and apostleship. All these aspects, which may be combined in a logical manner in theological thought, are gathered together in an imaginative and spontaneous way with the help of a single symbol.

The facts we have just established in this little digression may be applied profitably to the analysis of the various scenes in the account of the temptation.

Commentators on the text in question have often very rightly stressed that the motifs of the first scene, that is, the wilderness, Christ's hunger, the suggestion of the tempter to produce bread in a miraculous way, all recall the miracle of the manna in Exodus. On that occasion Yahweh satisfied the hunger of the people of Israel with bread from heaven. But because bread is a biblical theme which appears in other contexts in the Old Testament, we are justified in admitting other associations. Now the symbolism of the desert and of the bread in contrast to one another is characteristic of the account of the expulsion of the first couple from paradise after the fall. It is here that the curse on the earth is found: "Cursed is the ground because of you; in toil you shall eat of it all the days of your life. . . . In the sweat of your face you shall eat bread . . ." (Gen. 3:17, 19). We can establish that in the passages taken from the Old Testament, as in those from later Jewish writings which take up the theme of bread coming from heaven or the prospects of paradise to come, there is the underlying idea that the curse of the soil will disappear in the messianic era. This is why the repetition of the miracle of the manna is equivalent to the regaining of paradise in the light of the messianic hopes of the Jewish people. It is also from this category of ideas or associations that the symbolic signs of Elijah and Elisha draw their prophetic character.

If we look at the first scene of the temptation against a background of this sort it seems clear that the temptation has a messianic character. The creative act which produces bread in the desert cannot be considered solely as a means of stilling the hunger of an individual. By its very nature, and thanks to the associations it carries, it is a sign filled with messianic significance.

The associations which are inherent in the symbolism of the scene in question not only direct us to the Old Testament or to the eschatological hopes of the Jewish people, but also invite us to consider some passages in the New Testament where a similar symbolism recurs.

What is characteristic of Jesus and his preaching of the Good News is the parallelism evident in his words and his deeds, two components of his preaching and of his teaching which are inseparable from each other. His words not only express a message, for they are active and creative; they bear in themselves an authority and a power which not only surprise us, but which, in addition, change the state of things. The accounts of the miracles underline this importance of the words of Christ. This is expressed in a typical way in the request of the centurion of Capernaum: "But only say the word, and my servant will be healed" (Matt. 8:8; cf. Luke 7:7). Following these remarks, the words of the tempting devil take on their profound meaning: "Command these stones to become loaves of bread" (Matt. 4:3; cf. Luke 4:3). Later on we will point out the difference between the miracle which the devil wanted to bring about and the miraculous works Jesus himself accomplished. From the fact that Jesus refused to carry out the miracle suggested by the devil we may, however, note a certain similarity to his aversion to performing miracles just because his adversaries asked him to do so.

The first temptation of Christ is different from the temptations of Israel in the wilderness in that it is a question of the power of Jesus to perform miracles through his words, while the temptation of Israel bears upon the faith and confidence of the people. This again signifies that the temptation of Christ in its central structure has a messianic aspect.

We reach even more exact results if we examine the role played by the symbolism of bread in the Gospels. Regarding the question of method, we may rightly suppose that if Jesus had had the experience of a temptation which actualized the symbolism of bread, he had not been able to make use of his own part in this symbolism without making comparisons and distinctions. Similarly, the early church must have been aware of the associations and the contrasts involved. In the ministry of Jesus, apart from the fact that each meal may reveal a sense of community and an anticipation of the messianic feast, two scenes in particular make the symbolism in question stand out: the multiplying of the loaves (Mark 6:33–44; Matt. 14:13–21; Luke 9:11–17; 8:1–10; and Matt. 15:32–39) and the Last Supper (Mark

14:22–25 and Matt. 26:26–29; Luke 22:15–20). In these two events we find, on the one hand, the symbolism of the bread as a sign of salvation and, on the other, the ministry of Jesus, a probative and at the same time creative ministry.

The affinity of the multiplying of the loaves of bread with the typology of the miracle of the manna, as with the eschatological symbolism of the messianic banquet, has been pointed out in the commentaries. But a characteristic feature which is worth noting is that the picture of the good shepherd has been associated with all this by the Gospel tradition. Thus Mark says that Jesus, seeing the crowd that had followed him into the wilderness, "had compassion on them, because they were like sheep without a shepherd" (Mark 6:34). Jesus is thus depicted as a shepherd who gives to his flock both his words—"and he began to teach them many things"—and the material means of being able to listen to the Good News. These two aspects are constantly mingled with each other. Those who hunger and thirst for righteousness are satisfied with the words of Christ (Matt. 5:6), but those who are hungry in the literal sense of the word (Luke 6:21) also receive their bread. The synoptic tradition is aware of the fact that Jesus, thanks to associations inherent in his own manner of acting, can be depicted in terms of the good shepherd of Psalm 23. This is why the tradition says that he makes the crowds sit down on the green grass before distributing the bread to still their hunger (Mark 6:39 f.).

Being the good shepherd who gives his life for his sheep, Jesus blesses the bread on the occasion of the Last Supper in the midst of his disciples. The bread he hands out has become the true bread of life. For the true life can only issue from the death of the shepherd who gives the food. Thus the material bread, a condition of life and sustenance for all human existence, is transformed by the fact that he "give[s] his life as a ransom for many" (Mark 10:45). The Fourth Gospel, which puts the eucharistic speech after the account of the multiplying of the loaves, has clearly elaborated the connections existing between the miracle and the institution of the Eucharist, connections which are inherent, however, in the very symbolism, and which because of this appear already in the synoptic tradition.

What do these statements imply for the exegesis of the account of the temptation? If the devil wishes to persuade Christ to change the stones into bread, it means that the desert would be changed into paradise, which is none other than an eschatological miracle, an anticipation of the re-creation of the world. But if Jesus had succumbed to the temptation, he would have produced the miracle for himself ("he was hungry"). From the simple point of view of material existence it seems to be an important task to end the sterility of the desert and thus to change the conditions of human life. But it is necessary to pick out the theological meaning deriving from the fact that Jesus is presented as refusing this solution. This meaning is evident from the circumstances which characterize the miracle of the multiplying of the loaves. Jesus acts there as one who has pity on the multitudes. He is no longer alone, but he takes care of others who depend upon him. Further, when he blesses the bread on the occasion of the Last Supper, he does it as one who is going to give his life for men.

Thus we may say that the actual temptation consists in Jesus being confronted with the possibility of changing the conditions of life forthwith by a powerful and creative word but for his own benefit, without mercy or without solicitude for the spiritual and corporeal welfare of his brethren, without the decision to suffer and to give his life for the salvation of mankind. The solution Jesus chooses in opposition to the symbolism of the account of the fall of the first man and the curse on the earth and bread, is to admit the fact that only bread coming from the death of the good shepherd—and this means changed and re-created by redemption—can change the curse into a blessing and thus renew the conditions of human life. These are the implications of this same theme which Paul pursues in the searching account of Romans 8.

The second scene in the account of the temptation, according to the order in Matthew, which seems to be earlier than that of Luke, also raises questions as to its messianic character. There, again, we may see that it is first necessary to study thoroughly the analysis of the symbolism. The central point of the scene certainly does not consist of the devil wanting to suggest to Jesus that he make a demonstrative sign in front of those who go to the temple and consequently in front of the population of the Jewish capital. Indeed, in the text there is no mention of spectators. In another connection there is a certain importance in the fact that the scene takes place in the temple, the location of the presence of Yahweh among his people, the place where his *shekina* resides. It has been observed that the devil in taking Jesus to the temple of Jerusalem wants to remind him of his messianic mission. But it is precisely the true nature of this mission which is in question. It is possible legitimately to conceive of the temple in this scene as the house of the Father where Jesus should live (Luke 2:49). As we have already pointed out, the idea of obedience is dominant in the whole account. The proposal of the devil, suggesting that Jesus should cast himself down so that people would come forward to help him, seems to be difficult to fit into the framework of the typology of the march of Israel through the desert. The quotation taken from Psalm 91, put into the mouth of the tempter as the text stands, does not contribute to the elucidation of the problem.

But if the texts quoted from the Old Testament do not help, the Jewish speculations on the incidents of the march through the wilderness may furnish us with clues. If the theme of the temptation of Israel in the desert occurs several times in the Epistle to the Hebrews, this phenomenon seems due at least to a certain extent to the fact that the same theme was alive in the theological thought and in the learned discussions among the Jewish people. In actual fact, we can establish in some texts of rabbinic origin that the Jews were interested in the problem of the temptation on the fringe of the exegesis of Exodus 17:7: "And he called the name of the place Massah and Meribah, because of the faultfinding of the children of Israel, and because they put the LORD to the proof by saying, 'Is the LORD among us or not?' " It is precisely the episode at Massah which is the foundation for the verse in the book of Deuteronomy (6:16) quoted in the second scene from the account of the temptation of Christ: "You shall not tempt the Lord your God" (Matt. 4:7 and Luke 4:12). Now we find in the Jewish commentaries on this passage from Deuteronomy the following remarks: "They said: If he gives us food as a king, who lives in a town, so that nothing is lacking in the town, we will serve him" (R. Nehemia, Pesiq. 28a 1), and further: "Look at their folly: the *shekina* has taken them, they were borne on clouds of glory and surrounded by them"—an exegesis which is supported in the context by a quotation taken from Deuteronomy 1:31: "The LORD your God bore you, as a man bears his son" (Pesiq. R. 13, 55a).

With the help of these texts we may rightly suppose that the symbolism of the second scene is intended to express that Jesus had been tempted to be borne by the *shekina* of

God dwelling in the temple of Jerusalem, and this in a way analogous to the idea of the *shekina* bearing the people of Israel in the desert, which explains the somewhat curious fantasy of jumping from the top of the temple, an enterprise illustrated in the formation of our text by the quotation taken from Psalm 91.

But here, too, the symbolism is certainly more complex. The commentary of Strack-Billerbeck rightly quotes a passage from the *Antiquities* of Josephus in which the Jewish historian expresses the impression of immense depth which one has when looking at the abyss stretching below the south side from the top of the temple.[8] To throw oneself down would mean inevitable death. The reply of Jesus: "You shall not tempt the Lord your God" implies that he refused to abuse divine power to avoid death. It then follows that he accepts the design of God that the Messiah should suffer and die to enter into his glory (Luke 24:26). In these ideas as a whole it does not seem unwarranted to evoke as antitype the eschatological return of the Son of man on the clouds of heaven, surrounded by the angels (Matt. 25:31; Mark 14:62 and Matt. 26:64; Luke 22:69.

Just as in the preceding scene, no human being intervenes: this seems to have a certain significance. Further on in the synoptic Gospels we come to the miracles where Jesus appears as the one who dominates abysses and who conquers chaotic powers: there are the stories of the stilling of the tempest (Mark 4:35–41) and of the walking on the water (Mark 6:45–52). When the symbolism is compared, it is possible to establish certain likenesses to the second scene of the temptation. But the difference—and this is a point to which we have already drawn attention—consists in the fact that when performing the two miracles Jesus

---

[8]Josephus, *Ant.*, 15, 412.

not only shows his power to act and to anticipate the new creation, but that he intervenes to help his desolate disciples. When he accomplishes miracles, he does it in his mercy and as one who goes up to Jerusalem to give up his life.

The third scene of the temptation enters into the same category of ideas. It is probable that Matthew has preserved the original sequence of the scenes and that Luke has changed the order to stress the role played by the city of Jerusalem and its temple in Jesus' work. The messianic character of the temptation on the mountain is clearer. This mountain, which from the typological point of view corresponds to Mount Nebo in Deuteronomy 34, is conceived of as the center of the world and the point of departure for a domination of the whole world, a dominion reserved for the Messiah. Now the question arises: Who will give this dominion to the Messiah, God or Satan? It may rightly be asked in what measure such a question would be able to imply a true temptation for Jesus. It seems there is only one answer to this question. But the solution of the problem consists in the devil being prepared to give the kingdom and the dominion immediately, while God will not give them until after the suffering and death of the Messiah. For the third time it stands out that the central point of the temptation is not only the obedience of the Messiah, but obedience unto death. For the Messiah must die to achieve in its entirety the plan of God, to change in a radical way the conditions of human life.

That an interpretation of this kind may be warranted appears from an analysis of the symbolism of the mountain in analogous scenes occurring in the Gospels and especially in Matthew. As a counterpart to the mountain in the temptation we have the Galilean mountain where the risen

Christ talked to his disciples to send them out on their mission to the world. Then he can say: "All authority in heaven and on earth has been given to me" (Matt. 28:18). These words recall those of the tempter: "All these I will give you" (Matt. 4:9), but the difference does not only consist in the words "heaven and earth," indicating that it is God who has given him dominion. On the mount of temptation Jesus is alone with the devil; on the mountain of Galilee Christ is surrounded by his apostles who are ready to go out into the world to preach the gospel to men.

Golgotha is not a mountain, it is true, but we know that this hill entered into the framework of ideas which the early church entertained of the center of the world. And it was the cross raised on Calvary which bore the *titulus* in a symbolic way indicating the true character of the kingdom of Christ. The beatitudes in the Sermon on the Mount, as also the voice coming from heaven at the transfiguration, draw their deep meaning from the fact that Jesus has decided to be obedient until death.

If the core of the temptation consists in Christ having to decide whether he for his part accepts the road that leads to suffering and death, this implies that the account of the baptism and that of the temptation are bound together in an organic way. In the interpretations of the account of the baptism, one notices more and more that the symbolism there foreshadows suffering and death as forming a part of the mission of the Messiah. From the point of view of method it has been objected that the symbolic parallelism between the going down into the waters and the death, on the one hand, and the coming up out of the waters and the resurrection, on the other, are only found in the church fathers, while it is absent from Jewish literature of the Hellenistic period. This fact could indicate that this symbolism is of late origin and ought not to be introduced into the exegesis of the New Testament. In our opinion, however, nothing prevents the origin of this symbolism from going back to the teaching of Jesus nor that it was he who first combined the picture of the baptism and the idea of suffering and death. Thus would be explained the symbolism which comes back in a saying of Jesus which is certainly authentic: "Are you able . . . to be baptized with the baptism with which I am baptized?" (Mark 10:38). There is also reason to suppose that it is exactly these words of Jesus—or the tradition of a similar teaching—which have given rise to the theological thought of Paul: "Do you not know that all of us who have been baptized into Christ Jesus were baptized into his death?" (Rom. 6:3).

Thus understood, the account of the temptation has truly found its organic place at the point where Christ begins his messianic mission. The three scenes in their very structure express the fact that, from the beginning of his public ministry and following his own experience at the time of his baptism, Jesus has chosen the path of obedience unto death, which is that of the Son of God. It follows, according to him, that the messianic hopes could not be realized immediately. The way of salvation in this manner terminates in a deeper view: it is only through an obedience unto death that the conditions of life for the human species can be radically changed and renewed. Christ accepts suffering and death to acquire a kingship which guarantees the freedom of a new creation and a new humanity.

V. The Pericope *de adultera* in the Early Christian Tradition

Ever since the time when the appearance in print of the Greek text of the New Testament necessitated a comparison of various manuscripts, we have been aware that the account of Jesus and the adulteress in John 7:53–8:11 occupies a special position in textual tradition. It is entirely missing from the oldest and best manuscripts, and it does not appear in the old translations in their original form. Furthermore, it has not been difficult to show that the story, both from the point of view of content and stylistic form, does not fit into the Johannine framework: it breaks up the continuity of the Fourth Gospel and, by its construction and use of language, stands out as a peculiar insertion. Admittedly this phenomenon is not without counterpart in the text of the New Testament—we need only to think of the secondary conclusion to Mark—but this foreign element in the middle of the Gospel of John undeniably draws attention to itself. Now it is not our intention to try to explain why the story has ended up just in this place—which, moreover, is not the only one, since in a smaller group of manuscripts the pericope is inserted after Luke 21:38. The readiest assumption is that it was originally written down some time after the four Gospels, that is, at the end of a Gospel manuscript, and later inserted in the last of our Gospels in a place where it could conceivably be associated with the thoughts expressed there: there are points of connection partly in the words of Jesus to the adulteress: "Neither do I condemn you" (John 8:11), and partly in the words in John 8:15: "You judge according to the flesh, I judge no one."

More interesting, however, is the question: Where does the pericope come from and why has it at such a late stage crept into the canonical Gospel tradition?

Where does the account of Jesus and the adulteress come from? Exegetes representing the most widely differing views seem to be fairly unanimous in thinking that it must have had its origin in the same early Christian streams of tradition as those which have emerged in our synoptic Gospels. So far as concerns origin, both the content and form align the pericope with the material which we otherwise have in Mark or Matthew. We do not here have time to devote ourselves to a more detailed analysis of the account. Bultmann[1] regards the words of Jesus, "Let him who is without sin among you be the first to throw a stone at her" (John 8:7), as the apothegm, the pronouncement, around which the rest of the story has crystallized. In contrast, according to the form-critical classification of Dibelius[2] which here seems to fit better, we have rather a typical example of the paradigms: a brief complete account of a situation where the person of Jesus stands in the center, where the stress lies in his words and where the presentation results in a saying suited to preaching, in our case the admonition: "Neither do I condemn you; go, and do not sin again."

To summarize, the point of the story may briefly be said to be: only the Messiah, who is himself without sin, can unite radical judgment of sin with saving mercy toward the sinner. In a moment the woman's position has been changed —it holds something of the wonder of a new creation. Undeniably this story contains an element of the tradition of the early community and a picture from the life of Jesus;

---

[1]Bultmann, *History of the Synoptic Tradition*, p. 63.
[2]Dibelius, *From Tradition to Gospel*, p. 98.

and to this so to say synoptic impression the stylistic form also contributes: the particle δέ which carries events further from sentence to sentence instead of the Johannine οὖν, the designation of the crowds by λαός, where John would have preferred ὄχλος, the juxtaposition of "scribes and Pharisees," the mentioning of the Mount of Olives and such like. The sum of these various indications is that for excellent reasons one may consider the account of Jesus and the adulteress as a genuine early Christian element, and this we also intend to assume here.

If the pericope thus bears an original character, its late appearance in the written tradition is the more remarkable. At what time, then, did it make its appearance? In the Greek form we first find it in Codex D from the sixth century and thereafter in a number of representative manuscripts of the Byzantine form of the text. In Latin translation, however, it already appears sporadically before the Vulgate and then in the entire Vulgate tradition. Apart from Jerome, who claims to have come upon the pericope in both Greek and Latin manuscripts, it is mentioned by Ambrose and Augustine—while, on the other hand, earlier church fathers in the Greek and Latin language areas do not seem to know about it. Thus it appears toward the end of the fourth century, which may be worth remembering. However, we have signs of the existence of the pericope during the period when its tradition-history is otherwise wrapped in obscurity for us, and this may be a sign that the account is not a late product. According to a comment in Eusebius's church history,[3] Papias gave an account of a woman who was accused before the Lord for her many sins, and about this same story Eusebius says that it was also to be found in the Gospel to the Hebrews—whatever we may imagine this apocryphal book to be. With this we

---

[3]Eusebius *Hist. eccl.* 3. 19. 17.

have reached the second century. One step further forward in time, i.e., during the first half of the third century, a definite reference to our story is made in the Syrian *Didascalia*,[4] and this reappeared toward the end of the fourth century, this time worked into the Apostolic Constitutions.[5]

These glimpses in conjunction with the fact that the pericope obtained a footing in parts of the Western and Byzantine texts, of which the latter at least has Syrian origins, show that the account had in all probability hibernated in Syria. The actual text-critical apparatus to our story, with its many versions which are difficult to sort out, permits us in any case to understand that this passage was not included, when, about A.D. 200, various recensions, anonymous to us, created a certain order in the New Testament textual tradition. As these undertakings, especially the one which resulted in the so-called neutral or Alexandrian text, can most closely be localized in Egypt and Alexandria, we have at least one witness to the fact that the account of the adulteress did not have canonical standing in this part of the Mediterranean world toward the end of the second century.

What then is the reason why our pericope at this time and up to the fourth century is not to be found in the mainstream of the synoptic tradition? Whether it was found at a very early stage, we are of course not able to say. But why is it missing from about A.D. 150 until some time in the fourth century? Is it possible to think of any reasons why the story of Jesus and the adulteress was set aside and denied a place in the tradition and the versions which were canonized? Without doubt such are to be found. In all probability the contents of the account came to contrast in

[4]*Didasc.* 2. 24 (ed. Funk).
[5]*Const. apost.* 2. 24 (ed. Funk).

a disturbing and embarrassing way with the praxis of church discipline regarding offenses against the sixth commandment which naturally developed in the Christian communities; indeed, the first traces of this are already found in New Testament writings, where, for example, we can witness Paul's intervention in a striking case in Corinth.[6] Admittedly, so far as concerns the pericope *de adultera* we do not need to share Augustine's suspicion that anxious husbands had removed the account so that it should not be misused by their wives,[7] but the climax of the pericope, the words of Jesus: "Neither do I condemn you; go, and do not sin again," as time passed, must hardly have appeared to be in agreement with the way in which any regrettable cases of adultery were proceeded against in the communities. This disagreement must be thought to have led to more and more hesitation in quoting and using our pericope, which resulted in its slipping out of the mainstream of the tradition.

At what point of time should one then locate this change which resulted in a genuine Gospel story containing striking sayings of Jesus becoming inconvenient, so to speak, and being pushed aside? It must have been during the period when the Gospel tradition, which from the beginning had its *Sitz im Leben* particularly in the missionary message, came to be used more and more in the preaching within the church itself, when it was of course coupled with parenesis and ethical teaching. This development, which naturally started as soon as there was a Christian community life with its social and ethical problems, and which has to be considered in every study of the Gospel tradition, should have been especially noticeable during the first post-apostolic generation. Then one was faced with problems

[6] 1 Cor. 5:1 ff.
[7] Augustine *De coniug. adult.* 2. 7.

which distinguished the Christian communities from the messianic circle which had lived around Jesus: the church's representatives did not only have the task of showing publicans and sinners the way to a change of heart within the fellowship of the kingdom of God formed around the risen Lord, but they were compelled by a far from idyllic reality to take in hand people who, although baptized and belonging to the fellowship of the community, were guilty of sin, and, in addition, sometimes of severe and objectionable lapses. For instance, that they saw in the adultery of a member of the community a dreadful backsliding which brought with it judgment and condemnation appears, among other things, from some sayings of Paul in which the perpetrators of such sin are, on the one hand, excommunicated, that is, cut off from all fellowship with the community, and, on the other hand, are threatened with the loss of inheritance in the kingdom of God.[8] As an illustration of the attitude to sin committed by a Christian, the description in Acts of God's judgment on Ananias and Sapphira may also be cited.[9]

Nevertheless, in respect to the account of the adulteress it ought not to have been the contrast between the messianic mercy of Jesus and the radical condemnation of sins committed after baptism which made the account inconvenient. We must rather go a step further, namely to whether or not it was possible even for a Christian to receive forgiveness for sins committed and, insofar as he had been cast out of the community because of the gravity of such sins, to be received back again into the fellowship. Whatever attitude we take to the complicated question of the relationship between sinlessness and actual sins in the consciousness of the first Christian generations, it is inevitable that a realistic view of life must reckon with sin and forgiveness even in

[8] 1 Cor. 5:5 ff.; 6:9; Gal. 5:19.
[9] Acts 5:1 ff.

the circle of those who belonged to a Christian community. To quote Dodd's comments on 1 John 1:8 ("If we say we have no sin, we deceive ourselves"): "A Christian is expected not to sin. . . . The true teaching of the Gospel is, not that by initiation we become automatically sinless, but that within the Church we are under a dispensation which deals effectively with our sins."[10] Only the existence of such a view can be a reason for the fact that parenesis takes such a prominent place in the New Testament epistolary literature, even in the early Pauline letters.

But because the question of forgiveness of sin in the community became a live issue—and here it is necessary to remember that sin was not considered merely as a matter between God and the individual but, because of the strong feeling of fellowship, even as a conflict between the community and the doer—it brought with it an even stronger accentuation of penance as a complement to a change of heart and as a prerequisite for readmission into fellowship with God and the Christian community. Penance—which came to be an outward act of regret and submission—was not only some superficial disadvantage but a noticeable change of heart. The origin of the Christian practice of penance must naturally be seen against the background of the Jewish praxis of penance; there, there is already to be found such things as excommunication and readmission into fellowship, confession of sin, exercises in penance and prayer. It is not mere chance that in the Epistle of James, which belonged to a typically Jewish-Christian milieu, we find the first traces of a more pronounced Christian praxis of penance: "Therefore confess your sins to one another, and pray for one another, that you may be healed."[11] More

[10]C. H. Dodd, *The Johannine Epistles* (New York: Harper & Row, 1946), p. 22.
[11]James 5:16.

and more the practice of penance came into the foreground: beside the realization of the sin committed and confession comes *contritio* with weeping and lamentation in sackcloth and ashes and, in addition, all kinds of increasingly lasting obligations. The erring person was shut out from fellowship within the community. "With him who has sinned against his neighbour no one was allowed to speak nor shall he be allowed to hear anything from you until he has done penance," says the Didache.[12] The first Epistle of Clement already describes the outward procedure. Regret should take expression in moving prayers and in tears: "Let us fall down before the Lord and let us weep in our prayers, that he should be merciful and reconcile himself with us and lead us back to our modest and holy way marked by brotherly love."[13] Contrition and tears are, so to speak, the prerequisite for the intercession which is then held in the midst of the community for the one who has erred and fallen.[14]

An instinctive insight into how penance was regarded and how it was formed at a stage which naturally assumes a previous development, is granted us in the legend of the apostle John related by Clement of Alexandria.[15] The legend gives us a good idea not only of the apostle, but of the narrator's view of things. During a visit to a town in Asia Minor, the apostle entrusted a fine young man to the care of the bishop who was then there. The young man was educated and baptized—but, alas, evil comrades tempted him into the path of brigandage. When the apostle once again visited the community, he learned of the sad fate of the youth with the words: "He has died—he is dead to God." The old apostle then set out to seek for the renegade, found

[12]Did. 15:3.
[13]1 Clem. 48:1; cf. 51:1; 57:1.
[14]1 Clem. 56:1; 59:4; 60:1.
[15]Clement of Alexandria *Quis div. salv.* 42. 1–15.

him and persuaded him to realize his guilt with lamentations and tears. We particularly note that it says that by his tears he was baptized a second time. Nevertheless it was not so simple for the sinner to return. There followed a time of fasting, penance, and many prayers, when the repentant youth received help and guidance from his deliverer, the apostle, who did not leave his side until the change of heart and penance had been completed. We thus see that penance has become an institution and found its form—which in itself does not mean that Christianity had thus gone astray and sunk to a mere doctrine of good deeds. For usually one has a feeling that penance is not the means by which forgiveness is won, but an expression of the sincerity and tenacity of the change of heart.

Another thing is that the way back by penance was probably not open to all who had been shut out from the fellowship of worship and community life because of their offensive sins. Just as in the New Testament Epistles there are categorical condemnations of sinners and consequently of backsliders, so likewise there has been found in the post-apostolic period and in the early church a rigorous tendency not to want to accept any penance on the part of those who have been false to their Christian state. In drawing a distinction, necessary in practice, between forgivable and unforgivable sins, there were formed lists of vices, which vary to a certain extent, where those crimes considered as mortal were reckoned up, and such lists we recognize already in the New Testament. The motive for all such rigor has been associated with the view of baptism as the only decisive opportunity for man to become partaker in the immersion of forgiveness of sin.

In general, however, the development tended toward the differentiation and ever-clearer domination of the institution of penance. Montanists and Novatianists were not capable of carrying strictness to definite victory, and less and less were unforgivable sins mentioned. But it must have been just this development which made the pericope *de adultera* difficult to use in the life of the church.

Are there any points of comparison with the help of which we can check this surmise of ours?

Let us take a few random examples and see how during the first centuries in the early church those who had committed adultery were dealt with. The apostolic admonition that fornication and uncleanness—as befits the holy—should not even be named[16] understandably enough did not manage to hide the actual truth.

Hermas provides us with an example.[17] If someone has a wife who is a believer, that is, Christian, and finds out that she has committed adultery, does the husband commit a sin if he continues to live with her? So long as he does not know anything about it, the answer is, he does not sin. But if the husband finds out about her sin, and the woman does not do penance but remains in her fornication, and the husband then continues to live with her, he is a partaker of her sin. Further, it is asked: If the woman, after having been shut out (by her husband and, which is certainly implied, also by the community), does penance and wants to return to her husband, should she not then be received back again?—certainly, is the answer: if the husband does not receive her, he sins and brings down upon himself great sin. Thus the possibility of doing penance is evident, and, similarly, it is obvious that such penance attains its goal. Only the completely impenitent incur perdition—this is a thought which is also found in other contexts in Hermas.[18]

---

[16]Eph. 5:3.
[17]*Mand.* 4. 1. 4.
[18]*Vis.* 3. 6. 1; 3. 7. 1–3.

Or let us consider Clement of Alexandria,[19] which brings us to the period about A.D. 200. The Old Testament lays down that an adulteress is to be put to death. This was interpreted to mean that she who is guilty of fornication lives to sin but is dead to the commandments—that is, the interpretation is allegorical. On the other hand, the woman who does penance has through her conversion been born to a new life in that the sinner has died and the person newborn through penance has entered into life. This, therefore, means that penance should be looked upon as a rebirth analogous to what the New Testament says about baptism.

Cyprian, the bishop of Carthage who was active about A.D. 250, maintains that one should not exclude even renegades from penance. For the spirit of confession in the church does not need to suffer because one gives those who have fallen away—mostly because of fear—a chance to return, just as little as the purity of the church fails because adulteresses are given a time of penance and so permitted to gain peace. For there is a difference in having to wait for forgiveness as against immediately coming to glory; to be thrown into prison and not let out before the last mite has been paid and to receive immediately the reward of faith and virtue are not the same things.[20] Here we suspect something of the lengthiness and severity of the penances which clearly became more and more common in the church.

Against the background of the growing institution of penance, it is understandable to us that the account of Jesus and the adulteress could not very well be used as an example in the preaching and parenesis of the early church. What must have been embarrassing in this connection is, as we have seen, not the possibility of forgiveness: "Neither do

---

[19]Clement of Alexandria *Strom.* 2. 23; 147. 2 f.
[20]Cyprian *Ep.* 55. 20; cf. Tertullian *De pudic.* 13.

I condemn you; go, and do not sin again"—this matter, even so far as concerns apostate Christians, was discussed less and less as time went on. But, on the other hand, it was certainly not very easy for a teacher in the church to bring about, in connection with these words of Jesus, a lengthy penance with all its different stages and humiliations. So it happened that the pericope was left out—and this must have been just during the period when the church's praxis of penance was under discussion, took form, and was carried through with a firm hand, a process the beginning of which comes already within the New Testament period but whose decisive period must be put at some time during the second century.

Now it may be objected: why should just this particular pericope have been inconvenient, while the Lucan account of the sinner in Simon the Pharisee's house[21] is preserved by a unanimous manuscript tradition? Is there any difference? A hasty glance permits us, however, to see that in the Lucan pericope appear just such elements which must have made it especially suitable as an illustrative example. For there mention is made of the sacrifice of the alabaster jar, of the tears, of the kneeling position at the feet of Jesus. We remember the words: "But from the time I came in she has not ceased to kiss my feet. . . . Her sins, which are many, are forgiven, for she loved much" (Luke 7:45, 47)— everything which made suitable examples for penance. The sins were forgiven her because she had loved much, because her love and faith had saved her: the repentant sinner in the church of the second century could allow penance to become an expression of the strength of his love and faith. Thus, seen from the point of view of the problem of penance, there is an essential difference between the two New Testament accounts.

[21]Luke 7:36–50.

Now there remains still one further question. Why then did the account of the adulteress come back into the Gospel tradition? Textual history has shown us that this started to happen in the fourth century. And then there can only be one answer: at that time the church's institution of penance had gained such stability and self-evidence that the pericope could no longer give rise to obscurity and discussions. Now the Gospel account could once again fulfill a purpose without awakening surprise. It was still a good message, that forgiveness could be won even for such a sin as adultery, and now one knew that it likewise applied to the one who was baptized and Christian. But the church—perhaps not least after it became a state church under Constantine—had the care of souls and church discipline so firmly in its hands that forgiveness for postbaptismal sins without severe penance appeared unreasonable, and this meant that no one any longer would get the idea of interpreting the account in a way incompatible with this doctrine of penance. What was meant by the penance praxis of the time, at least on paper, we are informed about in the *canones,* which are included in the letters of Basil, the great bishop of Caesarea (d. 379): For fornicators the penalty is set at four years: one year they are to be excluded from worship and must weep outside the church gate, during the second year they have the right to listen, during the third to do penance, during the fourth they may stand with the congregation but without partaking of the eucharist.[22] For the adulteress up to fifteen years' penance is laid down.[23] Here a fixed and rigid order thus prevails.

To what extent church discipline had been stabilized during the fourth century with regard to the treatment of a person who had sinned against the sixth commandment

[22]Basil of Caesarea *Ep.* 59, can. 22; cf., however, can. 59.
[23]Basil of Caesarea *Ep.* 65, can. 58.

appears, finally, not least in the way in which there was a willingness to speak of the beautiful sinner's conversion and penance in edifying illustrative accounts. This sort of preaching was clearly first possible at a time when the danger of misuse and misunderstanding was excluded. In John Chrysostom, for example, we come upon a little story of this kind and there is nothing in itself which prevents it in its essence from going back to an actual event, even if it has been somewhat arranged with a pedagogical purpose in view. In one of the homilies on the Gospel of Matthew[24] we read—I give here a very brief outline: An actress in Antioch (known for its life of pleasure) who was rich and famous but notorious for her dissipated life, was converted to Christianity to the amazement of all. She gave up everything which had anything to do with her previous life, threw from her, as it says, the wiles of the devil and hastened toward heaven. As she had before been notorious far and wide, so she now became a model of self-denial and penance. The remainder of her life, during which time she also received the holy mysteries (baptism and communion), she spent in seclusion and in doing penance. This is the story and it teaches us how penance has, so to speak, self-evidently come to the foreground and, in this case, penance even for sins committed before conversion with baptism following only after a long interval of time.

A present-day prominent authority on legends has been able to show how this or a similar story was transferred and combined with a local saint of Antioch, a girl and martyr by the name of Pelagia, and, after this combination, how the legend about holy Pelagia's striking conversion and penance got into the world and was undoubtedly of edification to

[24]John Chrysostom *Hom. on Matt.* 67. 3 (on Matt. 21:31 f.).

many. Indeed, other legends of saints have been noticeably influenced in their wording by this version.[25]

To this may be added the observation that it was just in the fifth century that in the interpretation of the New Testament the sinner in the house of Simon the Pharisee began to be identified with Mary Magdalene. The first signs of this we find in Augustine and Leo the Great. Thereafter, the penitent Mary Magdalene becomes one of the most talked about and oft-depicted New Testament figures, a saint, around whom a flora of legend starts to be woven.

It is not only we who think we discern a certain coincidence and thus possibilities of direct associations between the appearance of the pericope on the adulteress in the New Testament stream of tradition in the fourth century and the origin and spreading of legends like that mentioned above. For when looking into the older Greek lectionary tradition and not least into the Palestinian-Syriac lectionary from the sixth century—which naturally reproduces a tradition somewhat older in itself—it is not without a certain satisfaction that we find that the pericope *de adultera* forms the Gospel text on Saint Pelagia's Day, October 8.

The circle has closed. The Gospel story, saved and preserved in unknown ways, when it came to light, has been combined at long last with a parenetically formed saint legend from a later period. The meeting between these two means nothing less than an extremely illuminating confrontation of two quite different aspects of the conception μετάνοια—conversion: on the other hand, in the biblical account, a momentous new creation of a human life through words of judgment and salvation uttered with the messianic power and authority of Jesus; on the other hand, the pedagogical depiction of lifelong regret and penance to

[25]Delehaye, *Les legendes hagiographiques* (1927), pp. 186–94.

attain the peace which is given by the same Lord and savior.

Thus the unique tradition-history of the pericope dealt with here has been able to throw a little light on the wider problem of the history of penance from the days of the ministry and preaching of Jesus to the great period of the early church in the fourth and fifth centuries.

VI. The Sabbath and the Lord's Day in Judaism, the Preaching of Jesus and Early Christianity

In the cultus of the Old Testament, as in the religious life of postexilic Judaism, the Sabbath is one of the most prominent institutions.[1] Besides the temple—which was locally bound up with the Palestinian capital and met with its definite downfall when Jerusalem was conquered by Titus in the year A.D. 70—and along with circumcision, the Sabbath remained inwardly a rallying symbol and outwardly a manifestation of the people of Israel and their piety throughout the ages.

We know that in New Testament times this seventh and last day of the week was encompassed by countless rules and restrictions, which are mainly collected together in the Mishnah tractate *Shabbat*. Their purpose was manifestly to preserve the holy character of the day and set it apart from the course of the other days. Seen from outside, however, the day received its distinctive character from the prohibitions governing the celebration of the Sabbath. Even in our own day within Orthodox Jewish circles the Sabbath is kept free from many of the tasks which otherwise form a part of regular everyday life. In the first century, as we see from the accounts in our Gospels, these restrictions gave rise to significant disputes and conflicts on matters of principle between Jesus and his opponents, the religious leaders of the Jews. In particular, when Jesus healed the

---

[1]"The Sabbath," in *Sayings of the Jewish Fathers*, trans. William O. E. Oesterley (New York: Macmillan, 1919); Paul Cotton, *From Sabbath to Sunday* (Bethlehem, Pa., the author, 1933); E. Jenni, *Die theologische Begrundung des Sabbatgebotes im Alten Testament* (1956) (*Theol. Studien*, 46).

sick on the Sabbath day it was considered an infringement of the character of the day, because even treatment of bodily suffering was looked upon as work and a creative contribution which conflicted with the purpose of the day of rest, namely, to bring about a break in human activity.

If behind the ancient and unique facade of the Sabbath a deeper meaning of its celebration is now sought, one finds not only a negative separation, but also a positive content, which in actual fact has always been current beneath the prohibitions and their minute detail. The seventh day serves as a constant and regularly recurrent sign—a reminder of the covenant that Yahweh has established with his people. Just as God is holy, so has every Israelite been called to holiness and sanctification (Lev. 19:2). But as these are difficult to combine with daily life, they are, so to speak, realized and take shape week by week in a rhythm which relates back to the account of the very creation and at the same time becomes an interpretation of it (Gen. 2:1–2).

Thus the Sabbath is a reminder of the creator and his will: "Remember the sabbath day, to keep it holy . . . for in six days the LORD made heaven and earth, the sea, and all that is in them, and rested the seventh day . . . and hallowed it" (Exod. 20:8, 11). But this does not only mean that man should worship his God by making use of the opportunity for worship which the day provides (Ps. 92); there also enters here something of the conception of the image of God, which constitutes a theme in the story of the creation (Gen. 1 f.). As God created the world in six days and then rested on the seventh, so is man to accomplish his work and purpose in this creation during the six working days of the week and then similarly rest on the seventh day. The purpose of this day is evidently not only for bodily rest or for a special object, namely, worship, but as the matter is expressed, or rather implied, in the texts (e.g., Exod. 20:11; Isa. 58:13 f.) it suggests a rhythm in life shared by Israel with Yahweh where the seventh day marks the surveying, the summing up, and the completion.[2] From these arise the Sabbath's character of joy and satisfaction, these also being focused on the thought of God's rest and pleasure. In a text from Hellenistic times this is expressed in a concrete way with regard to the Sabbath: "On that day they may eat and drink and bless him who created all things."[3]

Here it is in place to call to mind the role played in Jewish life, throughout the ages, by mealtimes on the Sabbath—particularly by the meal partaken of in the evening at the beginning of the Sabbath day. Here it is made evident that the Sabbath does not derive its character from special meetings or ceremonies, but from the content and character of a fellowship in the elementary social unit of the family during this particular day.

The Sabbath vigilance over rest and refreshment must, however, also be seen against the background of the Old Testament attitude to work, which is, in turn, a part of the great complex of Jewish anthropology. The commandment, "Six days you shall labor" (Exod. 20:9), is a prerequisite for the ideology of the Sabbath in the form which it has received; and even if man, according to the Genesis myth, has from the beginning been created to work and be active (Gen. 1:28; 2:15), human labor receives its true nature and interpretation in the narrative of the fall (Gen. 3:8–24), and in the curse which according to this story has been placed on the ground: "Cursed is the ground because of you; in toil you shall eat of it all the days of your life. . . . In the sweat of your face you shall eat bread till

[2]R. Guardini, *Der Sonntag* (1957), p. 11.
[3]Jub. 2:17 f.

you return to the ground" (3:17–19). In this attitude to man and his work the Sabbath supplies both refreshment and perspective.

As we know, already in preexilic times a distinctive phenomenon in Israelite thought was the focus of attention on the future and on the radical improvement in existence hoped for in respect to both the nation and the individual. People looked for the king who was to succeed in realizing the ideals to which experience had not even remotely attained, while at the same time it was considered that certain kings in the past—especially David—represented something of what they wanted to see in the leader of the people chosen by God for the future. Hastened by the harsh experiences of the exile and developed in increasingly detailed ideas during the period up to New Testament times, this eschatologizing also appropriated to its use the ideology of the Sabbath. The time of salvation could then be characterized, among other things, as an extended or prolonged Sabbath day: "When the LORD has given you rest from your pain and turmoil and the hard service with which you were made to serve" (Isa. 14:3). The theme came into further use in later times, when the Sabbath acquired an increasingly clear typological content foreshadowing the time of salvation, as was also the case, for instance, with the departure from Egypt and the journey to Canaan, the meanings of which were not only understood to be historic, but also to relate to the future. Thus it is said about the Sabbath: "As sleep foreshadows death and dreams prophecy, so does the sabbath represent the life of the age to come."[4] When "the time of salvation which is wholly sabbath and rest"[5] is spoken of, these two last-mentioned features were not entirely synonymous, for apart from

[4]GenR. 17:5.
[5]MTam. 7:4.

freedom from onerous work the Sabbath also meant joy and satisfaction.

The prospect of the messianic age also gave to the weekly celebration of the Sabbath a tone of glad confidence and hope wherever Jews gathered together on this day. The Sabbath was then said to give a foretaste of the coming age.[6] In this way in its ideology the day as a religious and national symbol became not only a backward glance at the creation, the history of salvation, and the conclusion of the covenant; it was also full of expectant hopes for the future.

The many limitations on individual freedom of movement which encircled the Sabbath easily lead us to believe that the day must have seemed heavy and dull for the people subject to the law. This was not at all the case, however. The general impression from texts and descriptions touching on the celebration of the Sabbath is that the day should above all be made festive. Not least was it forbidden to fast on that day. Even by dressing in the best clothes the day was to be marked out; sometimes mention is even made of white clothes on the Sabbath.[7] The fellowship, the mealtimes with the blessings and the breaking of bread, and the preparations, more or less elaborate according to one's means—these could then give a foretaste of the final perfection of creation and the end of tribulation. The Old Testament injunctions that servants and domestic animals should also be given their share in the Sabbath rest (Exod. 20:10) perhaps received greater stress in Hellenistic times than earlier because of the humanitarian elements which were more salient in the culture of that period than during ancient times.[8]

---

[6]GenR. 17; 44; bBer. 57 f.
[7]bSabb. 25b.
[8]Herman Strack and Paul Billerbeck, *Kommentar zum Neuen Testament aus Talmud und Midrasch.* 2nd ed.; Munich: 1954–61. See the Index and *Sabbat.*

This background should be borne in mind when one proposes to build up a picture of the attitude shown by Jesus toward the Sabbath. On this point, as in other cases where Jesus appears, we have to pay attention partly to his teaching and utterances and partly to his symbolic actions, which, not least where the Sabbath is concerned, have an essential significance when it comes to understanding the attitudes of Jesus. Indeed, it is by no mere chance that the fundamental features of the picture we get of his attitude to the Sabbath are the same as those which emerge in his attitude to the Jewish law as a whole. Here one may with advantage cast a glance at the problem of the Sermon on the Mount, although the Sabbath is not actually mentioned there. What characterizes the attitude of Jesus to the law is a peculiar, but in this case typical, dual approach. On the one hand, Jesus did not simply dismiss the legal tradition of his people, but found something God-given in it. It is therefore remarkable, after the recent discovery of Jewish sectarian writings, to be able to prove that Jesus did not belong to a sectarian opposition to official Judaism. On the contrary, he was loyal to the institutions which existed. We can see this, for example, in the way in which he took part in the services of the temple and synagogue or in the pilgrimages to the capital in connection with the main annual feasts. In his teaching he presupposes the validity of the basic commands of the law (e.g., Mark 10:1 ff.). But, on the other hand, while thus positively submitting to the forms established and laid down in the Scriptures, he implied in word and deed that he foresaw that the age of the law was drawing to an end and that it was his personal mission to lay the foundation of a new relationship to God and of a new worship sustained by his contribution. This is, for example, the meaning of the symbolism in the purging of the temple (Mark

11:15–17 and parallels; John 2:14–16).[9] Even the Sabbath became a *typos* in prophetic action consciously and consistently carried through by Jesus: it lost its character of an unchangeable institution in precisely those forms which it derived from the Old Testament, but at the same time it became a significant sign intended to foreshadow the new which was in the process of becoming a reality. Placed in a messianic setting the Sabbath was transformed so that it entirely pointed forward to a new order for the life of man. This transparent dual nature means that New Testament sayings and symbolic acts with the Sabbath as the theme should be analyzed partly starting from the traditional significance of the method of expression in the Old Testament-Palestinian milieu, and partly in relation to the entirety of the new message proclaimed by Jesus. It is therefore not difficult to understand that the attitude Jesus adopted toward the Sabbath appeared arbitrary and challenging to those of his fellow countrymen who did not believe in the claim he put forward.

The Gospels relate that on several occasions Jesus healed the sick on a Sabbath day: the man with a withered hand (Mark 3:1–6 and parallels), the woman with a spirit of infirmity (Luke 13:10–17), the lame man by the pool of Bethzatha (John 5:1–18), and the man blind from his birth (John 9). In connection with these acts of healing, discussions arose with the Jewish religious leaders, who branded Jesus as a transgressor of the Sabbath. From the accounts it is clear that Jesus did not act in ignorance of the law and its interpretations, but in full awareness of it. Admittedly, a certain elasticity was permitted in the Jewish observance of the Sabbath. In case of necessity, it was permissible to act as the occasion demanded and to come to

[9]A. Cole, *The New Temple, A Study in the Origins of the Catechetical "Form" of the Church in the New Testament* (London: 1951).

the assistance of people or even animals in need. Moreover, the various rabbinical schools, such as those of Shammai and Hillel, differed in the matter of strictness and liberalism in their attitude toward the application of the law. However, it would be wrong to assert—as is not infrequently done in commentaries on the Gospels—that Jesus intended to adopt a more generous and humane interpretation of the Jewish law, that he was a new, even more liberal, Hillel. In actual fact, there is nothing to indicate that on any occasion he wanted to take part in the discussion of Jewish law on its own level. His consciousness of his call was something different. From a formal point of view one can admittedly say that he kept within the limits of the Mosaic law, because as an adult Jew he had the right in a pressing situation to decide what due consideration for his fellow creatures demanded even on the Sabbath. But as a matter of fact Jesus did not dispute about details. He proclaimed essentials, the coming of the kingdom of God.

Therefore deeds of healing on Sabbath days must be interpreted as signs that in the person of Jesus was being realized something of what the Sabbath had pointed forward to in the eschatological expectations of the Jewish people; the message of the dawn of the time of salvation, of the fullness of life, of the new creation, received its expression in glimpses of none the less concrete manifestations and in symbolic acts where ordinary people weighed down by illnesses and infirmities could experience release from the shackles of their deformity and suffering. The problem is raised above the level of principles of law and patterns of action to that of the conditions and basis of life.

That we are right in adopting such a point of view toward these "Sabbath intermezzos" is evident even from the account of the plucking of the ears of corn (Mark

2:23–28 and parallels). Especially is this seen in the Matthean parallel (12:1–8), with its suggestion that something is taking place more important than the temple, which stands for the Old Testament relationship to God with its terms of existence. Jesus filled the occurrence on the Sabbath day with a comprehensive symbolism—unimportant in itself—when the disciples, to the angry chagrin of Pharisees who were present, picked ripe ears of corn while passing through a corn field. The grains of corn with which the disciples satisfied their hunger were suddenly set in relation to the bread of life which God would some day give to man in even greater measure than is the case with the harvest growing in the fields. The perspective in which Jesus regarded the Sabbath shows that the typological meaning of the Sabbath is superceded by its eschatological content, when it no longer needs to be surrounded by prohibitions and restrictions, but is rather filled with health, abundance, and the full possibilities of life for men, the lack of which characterizes their existence on earth. The Last Supper, which opens up the same eschatological perspective and to which, in its traditional wording, the account of the plucking of the ears of corn expressly alludes,[10] did not without a deeper meaning give rise to the generously inviting words "Take, eat" (Matt. 26:26 and parallel).

One may justifiably ask if the symbolism in the story of the plucking of the ears of corn does not consciously allude to a central theme in the account of the fall in Genesis 3. There the ground was cursed because of Adam so that he

[10]In the passage about the plucking of the ears of corn, as in the accounts of the feeding of the five thousand (Mark 6:41 and parallels; 8:6 and parallel), appear expressions for the distribution and receiving of the bread which are identical with the terms used in the accounts of the institution of the Last Supper. Especially in Luke's version (6:4) of the story of the plucking of the ears of corn does the reference to the behavior of Ahimilech (wrongly identified as Abiathar in Mark 2:26) use such expressions.

would be compelled to till it with the sweat of his brow, while the field of corn bore fruit for the disciples following Jesus without their having to labor. In that case, the associations of the saying of Jesus about rest for those who labor are obvious: "Come to me, all who labor and are heavy-laden, and I will give you rest" (Matt. 11:28 and parallel). The ideology of the Sabbath and its character experienced anew each week have thus been transposed to the eschatological level, definitive in the future, but already anticipated in the present. To the extent that the conditions of existence in the kingdom of God already break through in and around the messianic person of Jesus, so also will the situation and the experiences arising from that breakthrough be changed for the people who gather around him.

In the eschatological actualizing of the symbolic content of the Sabbath, when two types of experience in human existence confront each other, namely this age's negative experience of work and subsistence (which fills six week-days as distinct from the Sabbath) and the anticipation of the time of salvation with its security and peace, there is reason to ask if the typological antithesis Adam-Christ does not also enter here[11]—not only as a conclusion available to the present-day reader of the Bible, but as a theme already present to the mind of Jesus himself and the early church. In the conception of "the Son of man" in its New Testament form is also included, as an integral part of it, the motif of the new *Urmensch*. An example of this is the description of Jesus in Mark's version of the temptation: "And he was with the wild beasts; and the angels ministered to him" (1:13). One must therefore reckon that the term "man" in the logia which concludes the account of the plucking of the ears of corn: "The sabbath was made for man, not man for the sabbath" (Mark 2:27 and paral-

---

[11]Cf. J. Jeremias, ᾿Αδάμ, in Kittel, vol. 1.

lels) does not so much have a general meaning (= all men) but rather a typological meaning, namely "man," the new Adam or Son of man.[12] Through him the new content of the Sabbath, then, benefits the rest of mankind dependent on him.

The way in which Jesus placed his actions on the Sabbath and his utterances about this day within the entirety of his preaching about God's kingdom was naturally difficult or impossible to understand for the scribes and Pharisees, who could not bring themselves to break away from the basis of their judgment and habitual standards, that is, to undergo what Jesus designated by the term "rethinking" or "conversion" ($\mu\epsilon\tau\acute{a}\nu o\iota a$). As they saw the matter, the transgression of the law must be punished in order to safeguard what they considered to be essential in the Sabbath, what was laid down in the law given by God. When, however, Jesus made it appear that that same law had completed its function and belonged to the past—to be succeeded by a higher and a better reality—this revolutionary attitude was entirely bound up with the significance of his own person. The whole of his complicated, but basically superior, attitude to the Jewish Sabbath is one of the manifold expressions of an extremely intense, well-thought-out, and intellectually unified self-consciousness. Not only did the early church look back on Jesus as the Messiah personified, but he himself associated the Jewish people's messianic conceptions and expectations with his own person, and this in an extremely personal selection and in a very individual way. It is not surprising that his opponents misunderstood the symbolic references to the renewal of the creation and the fullness of life, when they in their stubbornness lacked the generous, humane, and liberating approach which manifested itself in the

[12]T. W. Manson, Mark ii, 27 f.: *Coniect. Neotest.* 11 (1947): 138–46.

Galilean prophet's way of using the Sabbath day. The radical and original element in Jesus' conception, however, is anchored in historic reality through the conflicts it provoked, which inevitably led to the death sentence against him. From our sources there is no doubt at all that the controversies about the observance of the Sabbath have their given place in this well-documented development of events.

If we now turn our gaze from the ministry of Jesus to the rules and conceptions of faith in the early church, it may seem as if the church should have retained the observance of the Sabbath—even though in a modified form—and this precisely because Jesus had given to this day a new symbolic content and consequently an eschatological perspective, something which must have appealed to the reflective activity of early Christian leaders. That they were aware of the Master's attitude to and teaching about the Sabbath is clear both from the fact that the pericopes containing the arguments concerning the Sabbath were handed down in the various strata of Gospel matter and also from the wording in which the various pericopes have been clothed.

However, the historical development was quite different. True, the apostles and members of the early congregation in Jerusalem continued to frequent the temple and the synagogue, above all certainly on the Sabbath, this being natural in the milieu in which they lived and worked. But the characteristic phenomenon was that a day distinct from the Sabbath, namely, the first day of the week, became the most important day of the Christian week and the chief occasion for worship. Now we can hardly think of the Christian life and the Christian celebration of worship without the fundamental and sustaining part played by Sunday, the day of the Lord, with its regularly recurring rhythm. The significance of this Sunday has, furthermore, been self-evident since the time of the ancient church.[13]

How has it come about that already in the New Testament period Christians made the day after the Sabbath into their special day for meetings and services? The usual explanation is that the early church chose the day of Christ's resurrection as its holy day, and, by pointing out the significance of the fact of the resurrection in this way, dissociated itself from Judaism, out of which the new movement had grown. As the main proof of this it is customary to quote the two statements in the Gospel of John that the apostles gathered on the first day of the week: "On the evening of that day, the first day of the week, the doors being shut where the disciples were, for fear of the Jews, Jesus came and stood among them" (John 20:19); and again: "Eight days later, his disciples were again in the house, and Thomas was with them. The doors were shut, but Jesus came and stood among them . . ." (20:26). Undeniably these words do not only contain what one knew of the events after the resurrection— at the time when the Gospel was formed—but they also reflect conditions in the early church when, as the apostles had done, people gathered together on the first day of the week in the private circle of the congregation, behind locked doors, something which grew more and more necessary as time passed and it became more dangerous to be Christian. So far the argument is correct. But what has not been sufficiently considered is that neither in the cited passages nor elsewhere is anything said about the apostles or later Christians in general gathering together on that day. True, Jesus had risen from the dead on the first day of the week

[13]Cotton, *From Sabbath to Sunday;* G. Schrenk, "Sabbat oder Sonntag," *Judaica* 2 (1946): 169–89; Alexander A. McArthur, *The Evolution of the Christian Year* (London: SCM Press, 1953).

according to Jewish chronology,[14] but if this day had been expressly selected as a substitute for the Sabbath by Christians, then somewhere in the New Testament writings or in the older literature of the early church it should be called "the day of the resurrection" or something similar. But all designations of this kind are lacking and, similarly, any suggestion in the texts in question that the early church consciously selected a week day for their gatherings is absent.

On the contrary, the fact is that the special day of meeting was called "the first after the sabbath," primarily in John 20:19.[15] When our Bible translation renders this as "the first day of the week" this is misleading insofar as the day even in its Christian nomenclature was still attached to the Sabbath. In the accounts of the resurrection in the Gospels there are no sayings which direct that the great event of Christ's resurrection should be commemorated on the particular day of the week on which it occurred. In these accounts and in the New Testament Epistles one rather gets the impression that the resurrection is dominating to such a degree that it appears more adequately referred to in the later wording of Origen: "For the perfect Christian every day is a day of the Lord."[16]

In actual fact there is nothing which indicates that the first weekday in the life of the early church was a "holy day" on an analogy with the Sabbath in the life of the Jewish people. A glance at the social circumstances permits us to understand that the small groups of people mostly recruited from the lower classes of society which composed the first Christian communities had no practical possibility of simply deciding to set aside a special weekday as their

[14]The day of the week of the resurrection is given in Mark 16:2; Matt. 28:1; Luke 24:1; John 20:1, and is thus well-documented.
[15]Τῇ μιᾷ σαββάτων.
[16]Origen *Contra Celsum* 8. 22.

124

holy day, turning aside from the daily habits of their surroundings. Such an assumption is unrealistic and also lacks support from the sources. The Christians had to follow the customs of their surroundings in the matter of free days, which meant that the Sabbath was their day of rest in the Palestinian milieu and the various festivals connected with local cults their free days in the Hellenistic world. Moreover, we have reason to reckon with a successive and—at least to begin with—unintentional development which gradually led to the time at the beginning of the fourth century when Sunday actually became the week's holy day through imperial edict.

The key to the solution of the question seems to be in the information about the life of the early congregation which is given to us in Acts. In spite of the later composition of this New Testament writing, we can, as is increasingly acknowledged by scholars, there find reliable traditions about conditions among the Christians in Jerusalem during the first decades.[17] About the members in the early church we can read that: "And day by day, attending the temple together and breaking bread in their homes, they partook of food with glad and generous hearts" (Acts 2:46). They therefore still took part in the services of the temple (and presumably also of the synagogues) and what Christians there would seem to have regarded as essential was the reading of the Scriptures and the prayers. Regarding the sacrificial cultus, the New Testament writings witness that the Christians fairly early came to understand that this had been replaced by Christ's sacrificial death and by his high-priestly function—maybe under certain influences from sectarian movements within Judaism which precisely repudiated sacrificial services in their official form. In this case the Epistle to the Hebrews shows an already

[17]B. Reicke, *Tro och liv i den kristna urförsamlingen* (Stockholm: 1958).

advanced stage of such christological reflection. The origin of a similar interpretation of Christ's death was also certainly promoted by the Last Supper, which in its actual institution and in the early Christian interpretation was associated with, and set up against, the sacrificial cultus and its central place in Jewish thought.

After the Christians had taken part in the worship of the temple, they gathered in their own separate circle, at first in the upper room (Acts 1:13). What took place at these private meetings is also related: "And they devoted themselves to the apostles' teaching and fellowship, to the breaking of bread and the prayers" (Acts 2:42). The picture which we thus get is peculiar in that the Christians, to begin with, did not give up the Jewish cultus, but so to speak complemented it. They continued in the readings from the Old Testament writings to acknowledge a holy word addressed to them, and they also continued to consider psalms and prayers as legitimate forms of worship.[18] But when they had done this, they gathered in their own circle in the consciousness that they there experienced the fulfillment of the Scriptures and the eschatological expectations. For there they came together in the name of him who himself had presented the Old Testament hope of a Messiah as fulfilled in his own person. That which was added when they were on their own was the recital of what Jesus had said and what he had done, accounts of how he had suffered, died, and risen again, prayers to him and in his name—to this belongs the exclamation which forms one of the very oldest components of Christian worship: "Our Lord, come" (1 Cor. 16:22)—and, finally, the celebration of the breaking of bread, the eucharist. This attitude to the

---

[18]Clifford W. Dugmore, *The Influence of the Synagogue upon the Divine Office* (New York: Oxford University Press, 1944). O. S. Rankin, "The Extent of the Influence of the Synagogue Service upon Christian Worship," *Journal of Jewish Studies* 1 (1948/49): 27–32.

Jewish service and its elements could be characterized by words from the Gospel of Luke, the speech of Jesus in the synagogue at Nazareth: "Today this scripture has been fulfilled in your hearing" (Luke 4:21).

When it is said that Christians in Jerusalem "daily" took part in the worship of the temple (Acts 2:46), this must, taking the actual conditions into consideration, be regarded as a hyperbolic expression. In all probability there were not so many in the Christian community who had the possibility of devoting all their time to worship and mutual fellowship. At the most this could be true of the apostles and a few in their immediate circle. On the other hand, we may take it for granted that the Sabbath days gave Christians in general the opportunity to go to the temple's or synagogue's three services during the course of the day, or at least to one or some of them.[19] During the following evening or night they could then go to the place where their Christian brethren, under the leadership of the apostles, met around that which was the essential in their new worship. Thus if the details in John 20 are put into the picture given us in Acts 1–2, it can be seen that the Christians' worship was not assigned to the day after the Sabbath, but rather to the evening of the Sabbath—and perhaps the night immediately following.

Such an assumption is in fact confirmed by the information we have in other connections in the New Testament. When Paul was in Troas and thus in a Christian community in a Hellenistic milieu in the fifties, people gathered together "on the first [day] after the sabbath" to break bread. From the context it appears that it was in the evening, perhaps late, for the apostle prolonged his sermon until midnight (Acts 20:7). It was on that occasion that a young man fell asleep and fell out of the window. The form of

[19]Dugmore, *Influence of the Synagogue*, pp. 11 ff.

the expression suggests that it was the evening after the Sabbath, not the evening after the day following the Sabbath. Thus the local Christian churches in the Mediterranean countries outside Palestine followed the customs which had arisen in Jerusalem of gathering on the evening of the Sabbath day. When Paul instructs the Corinthians that literally "on the first after the sabbath" they should put aside what they can do without to put in the collection (1 Cor. 16:2), it may be taken for granted that even in Corinth the Christians would not have had the possibility of meeting in the daytime, but it would appear to have been in the evening or night following the Jewish Sabbath. Not the day, but rather the night seems to have been the oldest time for worship in the Christian church.[20]

In texts of somewhat later composition it is mentioned that the Christian gatherings took place during the latter part of the night before dawn. This seems to depend on a continuous development, on a shifting from late evening to early morning. In his reply to the Emperor Trajan, Pliny the Younger, governor of Bithynia, thus writes: "They are accustomed to gather on a certain day before dawn and sing praise to Christ as a god."[21] This letter, written about the year A.D. 112, forms, with the quoted saying, a suitable background to what Ignatius of Antioch writes to the community in Magnesia in a letter dated at about the same time: "Those who lived according to the old order (= Judaism) have come to a new hope; they no longer observe the sabbath but the Lord's day, when our life arose (as the sun) through him and his death. . . ."[22] Here, at the beginning of the second century, exists a clear association of the time of the Christian service—assuredly

---

[20]Much later was the consciousness that Sunday in actual fact begins the preceding evening preserved in the church; see, e.g., Cotton, *From Sabbath to Sunday*, pp. 83 f.; McArthur, *Evolution of the Christian Year*, pp. 15 f.
[21]Pliny the Younger *Epist.* 96. 7.
[22]Ignatius of Antioch *Magn.* 9. 1.

in the rhythm of the week—with the morning of Christ's resurrection. It still appears that the Christians did not lay down any day for their meetings but were compelled to meet during a part of the night—at this stage the latter part—before sunrise. In Ignatius we now also come upon the expression "the day of the Lord (κυριακή), which he contrasts with the Jewish Sabbath. This is, however, the first witness to the fact that the Christian church had become conscious that its worship implied a new cultus in contrast to the Jewish observance of the Sabbath. It can also be shown that the expression "Lord's day" already discloses a consciousness on the part of Christianity of having its own "day." This expression is first supported in two cases, both of which are doubtlessly earlier than Ignatius: Revelation 1:10: "I was in the Spirit on the Lord's day" (ἐν τῇ κυριακῇ ἡμέρᾳ 1:10), and the Didache 14:1: "When you gather on the Lord's day (κατὰ κυριακὴν δὲ κυρίου) you shall break bread" (14:1). Moreover, insofar as one wants, in the details of the resurrection account in John 20, to find a conscious connection between the Christian gatherings and the day of the week of the resurrection, it should be remembered that even the Gospel of John was first composed toward the end of the first century.

Once the association between the meeting day of the Christians and the day of the week of the resurrection—or rather between the nights in both cases—had been effected, which probably took place toward the end of the first century, the way was open for the name "day of the resurrection." The instances of this name, however, are first found only in the second century.[23] One also still has to recognize that the actual day of the week for the major-

---

[23]Barn. 15:9; Just. Mart. *Apol.* 1. 67; *Dial.* 23. 3, 41; Clem. Alex. *Strom.* 7. 12. Cf. Peregr. Aeth. 24. 9 f. See also Cotton, *From Sabbath to Sunday*, pp. 81 f.

ity of Christians in the Mediterranean world's different countries did not differ noticeably from the remaining weekdays. To celebrate "the Lord's day" meant rather to sacrifice some of the night's sleep to be able to be at the place where the fellow believers gathered before dawn.

"The Lord's day" first became a true holiday under the Emperor Constantine during the earlier part of the fourth century. The necessary conditions for this were created by the recognition of Christianity as the official religion in the Roman empire. In the year 321 an edict was published which gave this day its position in civil life by declaring the Christian day to be the legitimate form of holiday with the status which the day of the sun had had within different cults in Roman life.[24] Thus "Sunday" had also been created, thereafter to become an inevitable part of the way of life in the Christian West.

The development which led to the official institution of Sunday was not entirely without complications. In spite of the emancipation of Christianity from the Jewish religion, the Sabbath continued to exercise a certain influence both on the practical celebration of the Christian day and on the formulation of the ideology of this day.

As the Sabbath in Jewish faith and life was one of the dominant signs of unity, so the relinquishment of, and the liberation from, the external observance of the Sabbath were an early event in the Christian church. There the attitude and dealings of the church leaders may be considered to have been prepared for by the teaching of Jesus and his symbolic acts, which could be understood more clearly after Easter and Pentecost and then interpreted as guides. In the New Testament Epistles a pervad-

---

[24]*Cod. Just.* 3. 12. 2; Eusebius *Vit. Const.* 4. 18–21. See also Walter W. Hyde, *Paganism to Christianity in the Roman Empire* (Philadelphia: University of Pennsylvania Press, 1946), pp. 257–64.

ing feature is that not a single positive saying about the celebration of the Sabbath in the Christian communities is to be found. While the commandments of the decalogue are otherwise referred to as valid rules even for the Christian life, the commandment about the Sabbath is conspicuous by its absence. On the contrary we see both in Paul (in the fifties) and in Ignatius (about 110) intensive efforts to prevent continued observance of the Sabbath commandment, and thus to prevent a relapse to Judaism. The circumstances were thus that the Christians celebrated their services mainly during the night following the Sabbath, but that they consciously repudiated the Jewish legal enactment which regulated the outward pattern of the Sabbath day.[25]

The fact that the Christian day—or night—of worship was preceded by the Sabbath, resulted, however, in even the Sabbath being used for Christian gatherings and services in districts where this day to a greater or lesser extent had the character of holiday in the general life of the community. It is easy to picture that for many members of the community it would be more suitable to take part in services during the course of this day, when work ceased in the large Jewish communities in, for example, Syrian towns, than to do this during the night hours before a new working day and working week. That this was the case can be read from the order of service in parts of the Eastern church, where instructions and lectionaries indicate that the Sabbath was a day of worship in a way similar to Sunday.[26] Here one must also reckon with a

---

[25]Col. 2:16; Ign. *Magn.* 9. 1. Cf. further, Just. Mart. *Dial.* 23. 3; Diogn. 4. 1; *Act. Petr. c. Sim.* 1; Iren. *Adv. haer.* 4. 16. 2–3. Jewish Christianity had its peculiar difficulties regarding observance of the Sabbath. This is presumably the background to Matt. 24:20. See also Eus. *Hist. eccl.* 3. 27. 5, and cf. Cotton, *From Sabbath to Sunday*, pp. 54 ff.

[26]Dugmore, *Influence of the Synagogue*, pp. 28 ff.; McArthur, *Evolution of the Christian Year*, pp. 24 ff.

certain ideological influence of Judaism on the church at a time when the church had become so consolidated that no relapses took place.[27] A superimposition of the Sabbath and Sunday took place.

Through the New Testament scriptures the Sabbath in the church maintained its typological significance, which in turn meant that the day could not fall into oblivion. That the typological interpretation, which gave to the Sabbath an eschatological significance in connection with the sensational sayings of Jesus about this day, was further developed in the early Christian observations and teaching is clear among other things from the reasoning in the Epistle to the Hebrews. There the salvation which Christian faith experiences and anticipates is described as the "rest" (κατάπαυσις) which God had made clear with the seventh day of the creation and with the entry into the promised land after the Israelite people's wandering in the desert (Heb. 4:1–13). In this connection apparently also belongs the interpretation which the Fourth Gospel gives to the words of Jesus: "For whatever he [the Father] does, that the Son does likewise" (John 5:19). This saying is here inserted in the discussion in connection with the healing of the lame man at the Pool of Bethzatha (John 5:1–18). Against the background of the Sabbath typology the utterance of Jesus receives the meaning that in the history of the world the time of God's creative activity is still going on, and that the eschatological "seventh day" still belongs to the future. This means that the history of the world is understood as a sequence of six "days" or periods of time, which will be succeeded by the time of salvation as the seventh complete "day." In this context the second part of the cited words of Jesus is to be understood: the life of Jesus

[27]Cf. M. Simon, *Versus Israel* (Paris: 1948), pp. 374 f.

and the messianic work of salvation still belong to the first six "days," the time of the divine creation, but at the same time are intended to make possible the coming of the "seventh day," the time of perfection.[28] Such a Christian typologizing of the week's symbolism is also seen later on in the writings of the church fathers. Bearing in mind that the fundamental Christian typology of the Sabbath was already to be found in Jesus, it is fully possible that the further development of these ideas, which can be traced in the Epistle to the Hebrews, continued further to the conception we found in the Gospel of John during the decades between the composition of the Epistle to the Hebrews and the Fourth Gospel.

It may thus be asserted that in early Christianity, on the one hand, people gave up the Sabbath in its Jewish form; but, on the other hand, they continued to operate with a Sabbath typology to illustrate Christian belief in salvation and hope for the future. That this double attitude could cause certain difficulties, not in practical church dealings, but rather in theological argument, is seen from a passage in the early church writing called the Epistle of Barnabas. This work gives us a good insight into how, in certain quarters, attempts were made to solve the question of the relation of the Christian faith to the Old Testament and Judaism. In a passage which has not yet received exhaustive treatment, this unknown author takes up the typological significance of the week: it reflects the millennium of world history according to the pattern, "For a thousand years in thy sight are but as yesterday when it is past" (Ps. 90:4).[29]

---

[28]O. Cullmann, "Sabbat und Sonntag nach dem Johannes-Evengelium," *In Memoriam Ernst Lohmeyer* (1951), pp. 127–31.

[29]J. Danielou, "La typologie millenariste de la semaine dans le christianisme primitif," *Vig. Christ.* 2 (1948): 1–16; A. Hermans, "Le Pseudo-Barnabe est-il millenariste?" *Eph. Theol. Lov.* 35 (1959): pp. 849–76.

We are there confronted with the following exegesis:

> Of the sabbath it is said in the story of the creation: "and on the seventh day God finished his work which he had done, and he rested on the seventh day and hallowed it, because on it God rested from all his work which he had done in creation" (Gen. 2:2 f.). Pay attention, children, to what this means: "He completed in six days" (*sic*). This means that the Lord will complete everything in 6000 years. He himself confirms this for me when he says "Lo, a Lord's day shall be as a thousand years" (Ps. 89:4 LXX freely rendered). Thus, children, during six days, that is to say six thousand years, everything will be completed. "And he rested on the seventh day." This means: when his Son has come and brought to an end the time of the lawless and judged the ungodly and changed the sun and the moon and the stars, then he will truly rest on the seventh day [Barn. 15:3–5].

Thus the author of this early church writing has given a typological interpretation of the Sabbath. The creation of the world and its history dominated by evil runs its course during six thousand years. The parousia of God's son with the last judgment and the transformation of the universe leads to the seventh (apparently unlimited) millennium, the kingdom of the Messiah or the time of salvation, which is characterized by true rest. In what follows the writer is anxious to draw up the Christian frontier against the Jewish celebration of the Sabbath in this age. He asserts that the Old Testament commandment about the observance of the Sabbath (Exod. 20:8), which belongs to the decalogue, cannot be carried into effect by imperfect people in this world and therefore cannot be intended to apply here in time:

> Further he says to them: "New moon and sabbath and the calling of assemblies—I cannot endure" (Isa. 1:13). Note how he says: not the present sabbath days are pleasing to me, but the sabbath which I have created, on which I accomplished the

134

whole and shall allow the eighth day to begin, which is the beginning of a new world [Barn. 15:8].

In typological fashion the author allows his thought suddenly and without obvious reason to glide from the seventh day as an expression of completion to an eighth day "never named in the quoted biblical passages," as a symbol of a new beginning, a new era.[30] The motive for this jump in thought soon becomes clear:

> Therefore we celebrate the eighth day as a day of joy, the day on which Jesus also arose from the dead and when he had appeared went up to the heavens [Barn. 15:9].

It is clear that the fact that the Christians celebrated the week's main services after the close of the Sabbath, at the beginning of the day following that day, did not fit into the typology of the eschatological week. Therefore a new typology was adopted, which could give a symbolic content to the Christian day of worship. But where did the symbolism of the "eighth day" come from? Clearly it forms a part of the meaning which in numerical speculation is assigned to the number eight, *ogdoas*.[31] Jewish apocalyptic at least gives us one instance where interest was shown in this number in connection with the calculation of time, and probably the representation of the eighth age as the perfect one has found its way into Jewish speculation from the East, from Mesopotamia. In the Slavonic Book of Enoch we read: "I have blessed the seventh day, the sabbath, and I have added to it the eighth, which is the first day of the creation. When the first seven days have passed as thousands

---

[30]H. Windisch, *Der Barnabasbrief* (1920) (*Handb. zum N.T., Erg-Bd.*), p. 384, has noted this jump in thought but has not explained it.
[31]See, e.g., Bo Reicke, *The Disobedient Spirits and Christian Baptism* (Copenhagen: Einar Munksgaard Forlag, 1946), pp. 140 ff.; *Reallexikon für Antike und Christentum*, vol. 1, see "Achtzahl."

of years then shall the eighth thousand years begin . . ."
(2 En. 33:1).[32] Characteristic of the *ogdoas* speculation is
that the eschatological perspective is more transcendental. In
the Jewish Sabbath typology, the time of final rest appears as
the fulfillment and completion of existing life and current
history. The way the symbolism of the eighth day has been
combined with the preceding seven as early as the Slavonic
Book of Enoch indicates an entirely new beginning. This
was a feature which came to be useful for the early Christian experience of the eschatological event. With the expectation of Christ's parousia on the last day is linked the
thought of the termination of this world and the appearance
of the new creation (cf. Rev. 22). In Christian worship and
in the work of the spirit, that which in its fullness belongs to
the future and a new world or age is already anticipated in
the present. Therefore the symbolic interpretation of the
Christian day of worship in the week as the eighth day
came to be a legitimate theme with the church fathers.[33]

The Epistle of Barnabas is not only the oldest example of
this interpretation. It also gives us, as we have seen, an
unconsciously clear picture of the problem which faced the
early church when it was a matter of combining the
typology of the week, in which the Sabbath was the suitable
symbol for the eschatological hope, with current developments in the life of the church, where for practical reasons
one was led to free oneself from the Sabbath. This difficulty is solved by the writer of the letter by means of a
tour de force, a jump in thought which helps him to preserve something of the Sabbath's symbolic content for the
Christian Sunday. However, this further shows that the

---

[32]Danielou, "La typologie millenariste," p. 3.
[33]See especially Just. Mart. *Apol.* 1. 67; *Dial.* 41. 4; cf. also J. Danielou,
"La fête des Tabernacles dans l'exégèse patristique," *Studia Patristica*
(1957), 1: 262–79, see 270 f.

combination of the first day of the week with the day of Christ's resurrection was not the primary and, from the very beginning, the ideologically dominating conception of the Christian day of worship, but rather that this had developed in obvious connection with the rhythm of the Jewish week but for practical reasons was postponed to the night after the Sabbath and later to the following day. Successively, therefore, Sunday was also filled with symbolic meaning, as the Lord's day, the day of the resurrection, the eighth day or day of regeneration, and finally the day of the sun.

VII. The Parables in the Synoptic and in the Johannine Traditions

In the interpretations of the parables of the Gospels during the years which have passed since the publication in 1899 of Adolf Jűlicher's great work *Die Gleichnisreden Jesu,* the connection between the message of the parables, on the one hand, and the whole of the ministry and preaching of Jesus about the kingdom of God, on the other, has been discerned much more clearly than was possible for Jűlicher at his time. The summary given in the synoptic Gospels of the preaching of Jesus in Galilee: "The time is fulfilled, and the kingdom of God is at hand; repent, and believe in the gospel" (Mark 1:15 and parallels), could also be given as a heading to the parables and what they want to express. In spite of the new knowledge with which the interpretation of the parables has thus been enriched, Jűlicher's contribution stands as a work which opened up new ground. He was the first who tackled what now seems to be an obvious and necessary task of exegesis when he made a clean sweep of the allegorizing which had dominated the interpretations of the parables during the long period since the days of the early church.

An example of what this allegorizing means may here be cited. In his comment on the parable of the prodigal son (Luke 15:11–32), Tertullian claims that the elder brother should be interpreted as the Jewish people, while the younger brother, the prodigal who returned, stands for the Christians. The inheritance which the latter received and squandered (15:12 f.) is the natural knowledge of God. The man in the far country for whom he worked (15:15) is none other than the devil, the prince of this world. The swine he was with are unclean souls. The robe the prodigal received when he repented and returned home (15:22) refers to the adoption as sons lost by Adam at his fall; the ring is the seal of faith through baptism, and the fatted calf which was killed refers to the eucharist.[1] This method of interpretation amounts to reading as much as possible of the Christian doctrine of salvation into a particular parable with the help of an interpretation of secondary details in the picture or story which, from the point of view of the text, is entirely arbitrary.

From such corruptions Jülicher led the interpretation of parables back to the essentials. As is well known, this German exegete maintained that every parable aims at expressing a single thought to which the whole picture or account refers. For the commentator it is a matter of finding and stressing this point and showing how the details, lacking significance in themselves, are subordinate to the main thought. Jülicher defined the meaning of the parable of the prodigal son in the following way: the way to the heart of God the Father is open even to the greatest sinner, provided only that he returns and receives back his sonship, without this meaning an encroachment on God's love of the righteous. For God it is a greater joy to forgive than not to need to forgive the one who is righteous.[2]

But as so often happens, the pendulum swung over to the other side, and it is therefore not possible to agree with Jülicher in the result of his interpretation. Would these incomparable parables have made the impression they did on their first hearers and on the many generations of hearers and readers since the time of Jesus, if their message had really only been that formulated by Jülicher in his

[1] Tert. *De pud.* 8 f.
[2] Adolf Jülicher, *Die Gleichnisreden Jesu*, 2d ed., 2 pts. (Tübingen: J. C. B. Mohr, 1898–99), pt. 2, p. 362.

more than meager simplifications? In actual fact these witness not so much to the spirit of the Gospels as to a bourgeois attitude to life in a German university town at the end of the nineteenth century. For example, the point of the parable about the talents (Matt. 25:14–30 and parallel) is said to be that faithfulness and diligence in work are necessary qualities for the one who wishes to enter the kingdom of God. Or, again, the parable of the rich fool who pulled down his barns to build larger ones (Luke 12:13–21) was to teach that even the richest of men is dependent on God's mercy.

Nowadays it is not difficult to see that such interpretations are to a great extent connected with the age in which they arose and that they are based on a conception of the person and preaching of Jesus which is not borne out by the sources. The picture of Jesus as a philosopher who appeared sublime to the bourgeoisie at the end of the last century had been created by an arbitrary choice of fragments of what is in the Gospels. We regard the parables and their message more realistically when we place them in the setting of the whole of Jesus' extremely characteristic, yet also pointed and shocking, preaching about the crisis which the imminent coming of God's kingdom brings for mankind and for the individual. The parables were much more charged with meaning than Jülicher ever realized. Let us remember that among other things it was the parable of the prodigal son which provoked the embittered reaction among Jesus' leading fellow countrymen and which became the immediate cause of his death. Were two world wars necessary, we may wonder, for the exegetes to learn to understand that Jesus was not a philosopher who with timeless pedagogy scattered aphorisms about, but that he identified himself with a message which was as urgent as it was unexpected?

The important works of C. H. Dodd *(The Parables of the Kingdom,* 1935) and of J. Jeremias *(Die Gleichnisse Jesu,* 1947)[3] have pointed out the eschatological outlook in the preaching of Jesus and thus also in his parables. The kingdom of God is not the result of an imminent development of the world and humanity but awaits us as a revolutionary event to come through the intervention of God in the course of history. Therefore the parables do not express any general truths but describe the unexpected which happens when the kingdom of God dawns. And he who formulates and makes known the parables is in his own person a sign that the kingdom of God is at hand and is taking shape.

This aspect appears clearly in Dodd's interpretation of the parable of the prodigal son, essentially briefer than Jülicher's circumstantial interpretation but at the same time more profound: the ministry of Jesus means the coming of God's kingdom; one of the events which characterized this coming was solicitude on behalf of the "prodigals," this being quite unparalleled.[4] Jeremias further says more precisely: the parables have two "peaks"; the main significance rests in such cases on the second. The meaning is then that the love of God appears precisely in joy at the return of the prodigal. But as this has become a reality through the coming of Jesus, the scribes and Pharisees should not show rancor but partake in the rejoicing. The parable is thus directed to those who look critically on the preaching ministry of Jesus in order to defend the joyful message of the gospel.[5]

The coming of the kingdom of God in the preaching ministry of Jesus and the consequences which this coming

---

[3]Eng. trans., *The Parables of Jesus,* trans. S. H. Hooke (New York: Charles Scribner's Sons, 1955).
[4]Dodd, *Parables of the Kingdom,* p. 120.
[5]Jeremias, *Parables of Jesus,* pp. 103 f.

brings with it for men thus forms the theme in the parables which have been chiefly preserved for us in the synoptic tradition. What they want to say, for example—to take the parable of the sower (Mark 4:3–8 and parallels)–is that what started quite insignificantly around the person of the Galilean preacher would develop into an overwhelmingly powerful result. In an inexplicable way the seed in the field grows into a harvest which is enormous in relation to what appears to have been put in, so that the picture, as Jeremias has shown (p. 92), is of a yield which is not only reckoned in relation to that part of the field which happened to be fertile, but in relation to the whole field, thus further bringing out the paradox in the presentation.

But if the time in the parables of Jesus is represented as being fulfilled so that the kingdom of God is in the process of dawning, this means at the same time that judgment is at hand, the day of the Lord which has formed an important and well-known motif in the religious conception of the Jews ever since the days of the Old Testament prophets. The signs of the times indicate a crisis and a catastrophe: it is a matter of considering the consequence (Luke 12:54–56). The people who do not listen, presented in the picture of an unfruitful fig tree, a formation from the motif of the tree of life (Luke 13:6–9; cf. Mark 11:13 f., 20 f., and parallel), will be judged. Therefore the seriousness of the situation demands that mankind stake everything on one throw of the dice (as, for example, the parable of the unrighteous steward who knew how to act wisely— from his way of looking at things [Luke 16:1–8]), turn around (in its way of life) and become as a child, in order to be able to enter the kingdom of God (Matt. 18:3). Here it is a question of the conception "change of mind" or "conversion" (μετάνοια).

The demand for such a reorientation of one's whole way

of thinking also discloses an essential feature in the message of Jesus and this not least in the parables. These parables are admittedly simple and striking in their choice of motif and their formation, but in spite of their pedagogical clarity they cannot be understood by a person who is not ready to throw all habitual values overboard and quite simply rely on the new context which is suggested and personified by him who propounds the parables. Here it again becomes clear that Jülicher's interpretation of the parables was in error when he worked with generally available truths and maxims as containing their message. Rather, the understanding of the contents of the parables is indissolubly bound up with the hearer's attitude to the person of Jesus and dependent on belief in his words. The characteristic description of Jesus and his ministry preserved in the Gospel tradition, namely that he "taught them as one who had authority, and not as the scribes" (Mark 1:22 and parallels), says something essential even about the prerequisites for an understanding of his parables. The opposite to such understanding, which builds on trust in the person of Jesus and what appears with him, is "hardness of heart," a notion which was also the object of reflection at an early stage (Mark 4:11 f. and parallels).

Since the work of Dodd and Jeremias, the organic position of the parables in the preaching and teaching of Jesus as a whole stands out more clearly. However, there exist not only problems of detail, but also constant questions about the exegesis of the parables which require further penetration. Above all this applies to the problem of allegory. From the purely exegetical-historical point of view it may be said that Jülicher's attitude seems somewhat exaggerated—his pouring of ridicule on the allegorizing interpretations which have appeared throughout the history of the church and the history of the interpretation of the manuscripts. Partly, there should in no small measure have been the recognition that allegory has been used as an over-interpretation for edifying purposes, and partly that allegorizing resulted de facto in the inclusion of the message of the different parables in the Gospels' preaching of salvation as a whole. Basically the above-mentioned interpretation of the parable of the prodigal son in Tertullian does more justice to the parable's original contents than Jűlicher's jejune interpretation. Therefore it may be justifiable to tone down to some extent the usual, haughty dismissal of the allegorizing interpretation in present-day works on the parables and instead to try to understand the purpose of the allegory. We may then see that during a long period this method formed a sort of secondary shell which nevertheless kept the kernel of the parables intact. For the present-day exegete it is naturally necessary to remove this shell to let the kernel appear to advantage. Thus Jűlicher did make a lasting contribution when he weeded the overgrown garden of the interpretations of the parables and freed it from a tangle of wild allegorizing, even if it may now be said in retrospect that in his enthusiasm for research he went so far that the result was devastating.

But the question of the role of allegory in the parables is not solved by pruning the imaginative blooms of the church fathers away from legitimate exegesis. For various allegorical features are found in the text of the parables as they stand in our Gospels. This is a phenomenon which, naturally, even Jűlicher had reason to observe and draw conclusions from. The typical example for the method which was most radically practiced by Jűlicher is the interpretation of the parable of the sower (Mark 4:3–8, 14–20, and parallels). It is inevitable that the interpretation of the parable which the Gospels already give and which they put into the mouth of Jesus (4:14–20 and parallels) contains allegorizing features, because various details in the picture and story, namely the sower and the various parts of the field, are said to "mean" something special in the sphere of experience to which the gospel message belongs. This resulted in the interpretation of the parable given by the Synoptics being declared secondary, that is, not created by Jesus, but by Christians in the apostolic age, who in a meddlesome way had put their own thoughts and experiences into the original parable and thus spoiled its simple purity.[6]

Even if Jeremias does not proceed so much like a schoolmaster as Jülicher, and even if—thanks to his great familiarity with Palestinian ways of thought and expression—he reaches essentially more diversified conclusions, his exegesis builds largely on the supposition that it should be possible to distinguish the parables or parts thereof—with the absence of allegorizing features as a criterion—in which we are confronted by the authentic message or teaching of Jesus, *ipsissima vox Iesu*. In various cases it is also evident, and therefore acknowledged by most commentators, that the expansions or alterations in the parables—that it is a question of such most often appears from a synoptic comparison—are secondary, and that they have a predeliction for allegory. As an illustration, the small changes which in Matthew and Luke have made their way into the parable of the wicked servants in the vineyard (Mark 12:1–11; Matt. 21:33–44; Luke 20:9–18) may here be cited. In Matthew the little story has thus become a concentrated compendium of the history of salvation in which the servants of the owner of the vineyard, who are sent out in two parties, represent the earlier and the later prophets whose fate is hinted at, and in which the conclusion of the story points toward the mission

[6]Jülicher, *Die Gleichnisreden Jesu*, pt. 1, pp. 60 ff.

to the heathen as a result of Israel's disobedience. Further, both in Matthew and Luke a rearrangement has been made of what happened to the son sent out: in Luke he was thrown out of the vineyard and then killed, while in Mark he was killed in the vineyard and his dead body was thrown out. In this case it is quite clear that the death of Jesus outside Jerusalem is the reason for the changes made.

But how about the main motif, the son who was sent to the vineyard and there loses his life? Jeremias emphatically declares that it is not a question of an allegory but of a parable which Jesus related in connection with some concrete event which happened and was talked of. The German exegete wants thus to preserve the parable as authentic, even if he is compelled to admit that the express linking up of the vineyard motif to Isaiah 5 means a sort of allegorizing.[7] But in the son Jesus could not have alluded to himself, for in such case an allegory would exist, and this must not be the case.

As distinct from radical critics and skeptics, as for example Rudolf Bultmann in his *Geschichte der synoptischen Tradition*,[8] Jeremias considered the main part of the parable material of the synoptic Gospels as authentic, after it had been purged of certain excrescences. This presupposes that the motifs are "deallegorized." Jeremias also carries this program out with respect to the parable of the ten virgins, about which he asserts that the bridegroom in the story does not refer to Jesus—or, more generally, to the Messiah —since the equation "bridegroom = Messiah" is not borne out in Jewish literature. On the other hand, the interpretation of the parable of the tares among the wheat (Matt. 13:24–30, 36–43) is considered as a clear allegorizing and, therefore, later addition, which—as the vocabulary shows—

[7] Jeremias, *Parables of Jesus*, pp. 55 f.
[8] Eng. trans., *History of the Synoptic Tradition*, see p. 4, n. 1, above.

has been written and added to the original parable by Matthew himself.[9]

When it is thus held that every trace of allegory constitutes an indication that a parable or a part of one cannot have been presented by Jesus himself but must be classified as secondary, then there is reason to ask if the criterion thus used really answers to the material. The difference between simile, metaphor, and allegory, which Jülicher and Bultmann work with and which Jeremias has taken over without renewed examination, builds on Western distinctions whose appropriateness to the biblical parable material may be questioned, as Jülicher is already compelled to admit in several places in his great work. The investigation of the use and form which the figure of speech, *mašal*, has in the Old Testament and in Jewish literature shows, rather, that the limits between simile, metaphor, and allegory are extremely vague, and, above all, that in Semitic literature it belongs to the nature of the figure of speech that we are there concerned with modifications, associations, and allusions. A study of these phenomena appears in the great work of M. Hermaniuk.[10] Furthermore, it is characteristic that neither Jülicher nor Jeremias has gone into the Old Testament background of the parables of the Gospels. It therefore appears legitimate to ask, as a question of principle, if in the Palestinian way of presentation at the time of Jesus there existed such a difference between what we call "pure comparison," on the one hand, and allusive metaphors or allegorical symbolism, on the other. Can this difference be taken as a basis for determining what Jesus said and what he cannot have said? There is further reason to ask how it is to be explained that Jesus did not make use of—or perhaps directly avoided—the means of expression of the allegory,

[9] Jeremias, *Parables of Jesus*, pp. 64 ff.
[10] M. Hermaniuk, "Le monde semitique," *La Parabole evangelique* (1947), pp. 62–192.

when even his disciples and the Christians behind the present form of the Gospels were apparently supposed to have made quite evident use of these means. To this last question, by using Jülicher's arguments, we may admittedly reply that the feature of the parables is simplicity, while allegory is more complicated. But nowadays we know that the category of "simplicity" belongs to a picture of Jesus which for historical-critical reasons has been abandoned. Still, however, in Jeremias the analysis of the parables builds on the unexpressed presupposition that "the voice of Jesus himself" is characterized by a simplicity and a single-mindedness which could almost be called one-sided, while the multiplicity of thoughts and experiences which the early church, according to the same scholar, has associated with the parables is regarded simply as a "defection" from the "purity" which has been taken for granted as the original. Literary-historical, ideo-historical, or psychological arguments for the claimed fundamental change which is supposed to have taken place between the teaching of Jesus and that of early Christianity have never been put forward, but rather only a series of theological arguments, such as the delay of the parousia, the missionary situations, or the catechetical need. However, these arguments do not carry weight and do not therefore permit unequivocal determination, and they consequently remain uncertain and subject to the influence of preconceived ideas.

As we all know, the rediscovery of the Old Testament background has been extremely fruitful for the understanding of the New Testament texts and not least the Gospels and their picture of Jesus. A milestone in this development which has taken place during recent decades is formed, as is known, by Sir Edwyn Hoskyns's book, *The Riddle of the New Testament* (see p. 150, n. 11), which is also a sign that English scholars have been in the lead in the field of

New Testament scholarship. Hoskyns has in a pioneering way made clear that the pictures which Jesus used in his parabolic teaching not only deal with events and situations of daily life in the Palestinian countryside, but consciously take up metaphorical ways of expression and conceptions which were traditional in Old Testament literature and thus familiar to the listeners Jesus addressed. In connection with a recapitulation of the motif "sowing and harvesting," Hoskyns thus quotes a whole series of quotations from the Psalms and the books of the prophets, from which it appears that the mutually connected pictures of the sowing and the gathering of the harvest have been used to express the conceptions of the saving acts of Yahweh in history and of the coming of the End of the Days. When Jesus makes use of the same motif in the parable of the sower or in the parables which are related by motif, he does not, however, reproduce Old Testament statements but presents pictures with a spontaneity and a freshness which have taken their colors from the visible reality around him. It is not book learning, but an observant eye which has provided the contours for these parables. But at the same time the motif or theme must have seemed well-known to the listeners. Those who knew their Holy Scriptures could not avoid thinking of what Isaiah (32:13 ff.; 55:10 f.) or Jeremiah (31:27 f.; 51:33) or Hosea (2:21 ff.; 6:11) had said of the sowing which Yahweh would bring to harvest in "that day," and for him who sees these obvious connections it becomes clear that it belongs to the message of the parables that what is hinted at in the Old Testament texts is now actualized through the message in the service of which the parables were uttered.[11] Already the choice of motif in actual fact shows that "the time is fulfilled."

[11]Edwyn Hoskyns and F. N. Davey, *The Riddle of the New Testament* (3rd ed.; Faber & Faber, 1947), pp. 130 ff.

Let us take another example. The parable of the lost sheep (Luke 15:4–7; cf. Matt. 18:12–14) clearly describes a situation which could occur in the activity of an ordinary shepherd in the barren mountain districts of Judaea or Galilee. But inasmuch as we have learned that one of the animals has run away, the basis of reality, so to speak, comes to an end. For the whole point of the parable is that the shepherd did not act as he should have if he had been experienced. In that case he would not have left the ninety-nine even if one of the sheep had unfortunately gone astray. Seen from the experiences of everyday life the "message" of the parable is thus nonsense, and therefore the audience must have been stirred to think that this strange preacher came with something which was different and divergent from ordinary conceptions and patterns of behavior. No, the parable hardly deals with the practice of rational sheep-raising, but with the help of a picture which was apparently an everyday one, it puts forward in quite obvious metaphors or symbols a conception of shepherd and sheep which must have been well-known to Galilean listeners from characteristic texts in the Old Testament, for example, Psalm 23 ("The Lord is my shepherd") or Ezekiel 34 (the oracle of judgment against the bad shepherds of Israel and the oracle of promise that Yahweh will be a good shepherd to the people)—to mention only some of the passages where the motif occurs. What is more, in the quoted chapter from Ezekiel stands the statement: "I will seek the lost, and I will bring back the strayed" (34:16). It is scarcely possible to avoid seeing a conscious allusion in the parable itself to this Old Testament passage.

Faced with such observations one begins to see that the parables are admittedly molded in one piece and manifestly in a way which reveals that they are not the product of study, but the work of a fresh creative personality, and that

they are at the same time somewhat more complicated than
Jűlicher believed or than Jeremias is yet prepared to admit.
In the actual choice of motif lie allusions and clearly conscious associations which inevitably bring into the pictures
and comparisons used metaphorical and allegorical features.
Behind the anonymous shepherd in the parable may be
glimpsed Yahweh, whose eschatological action described in
Ezèkiel 34 takes form in the glad tidings of Jesus to publicans and sinners. He has come to take compassion on them
"because they were like sheep without a shepherd" (Mark
6:34). We therefore consider it possible to establish that
the parables to an important extent build on a choice of
picture, symbolism, or motifs which may be represented as
filled with associations or which are "religiously charged,"
because of their obvious affinities with Old Testament texts
and thus with a conception of the world traditional in the
Palestinian milieu.

In one respect this peculiarity may be further elaborated.
The picture of the bridegroom who appears in the sayings
of Jesus in some passages in the Gospels has caused certain
difficulties. We have the saying about the wedding guests
who cannot fast as long as the bridegroom is with them
(Mark 2:19 f.); and again the bridegroom appears, as we
know, in the parable of the ten virgins (Matt. 25:1–13).
That Matthew already allows the figure of the bridegroom
to refer to Christ is clear,[12] and this shows that the interpretation in question was current in the early church. Now
Jeremias wants to claim that the figure of the bridegroom
admittedly belongs to the original parable of the virgins and
that this goes back to Jesus himself. But from the beginning
the bridegroom did not have any allegorical content, that is,
no reference to Jesus or the Messiah, but was entirely of
secondary importance in the picture of the actual wedding.

[12]See Jeremias, *Parables of Jesus*, pp. 41 f.

The reason for this supposition is that the metaphor "bridegroom = Christ" first comes in 1 Corinthians 11:2 and in the secondary verse Mark 2:20; but above all the combination of "Messiah = bridegroom" is not borne out, either in the Old Testament or in Judaism up to New Testament times. This line of argument is typical, but in no way invulnerable. When Christ is represented as bridegroom in any case in at least two passages in the New Testament, what is there to say that this combination has been created by a Paul or by the tradition before Mark, but that Jesus cannot have been responsible for it? When it is a question of the message of the parables, Jesus is represented as so original that, as distinct from his disciples, he can keep the parables completely free from allegories. When again it is a question of the bridegroom as a symbol for the Messiah, Jesus could not have used this because the combination is not found before him. In actual fact, there is reason to suppose that it was none other than Jesus who made this combination. We know it is characteristic of his self-consciousness that he applied to his person categories which in the Old Testament were reserved for Yahweh himself. This observation has been more closely followed up by E. Stauffer in his books on Jesus, even if he undeniably goes too far in claiming that Jesus did not at all want to be the Messiah, but rather God. But when, for example, Jesus forgave sins (Mark 2:5 ff.), he without doubt laid claim to a privilege which according to Jewish ideas was exclusively reserved for Yahweh and could not even be granted to the Messiah. Under these circumstances it is sufficient to be able to show that in the Old Testament and later Jewish conceptions Yahweh had been likened to a bridegroom. This is not difficult to do: it should here be sufficient to refer to such texts as the royal Psalm 45, and further Hosea 2; Ezekiel 16, and the Song of Songs. From these starting points it is at least conceivable that, in the parable of the ten virgins, Jesus allowed the figure of the bridegroom to be a symbol for his own person.

When it has become clear that the pictures in the Gospels' parables, as a result of conscious allusions to Old Testament texts and representations, may be "religiously charged," it is not possible to follow entirely in Jeremias's (and consequently also Jűlicher's) footsteps on the way to a complete "deallegorizing" of interpretation. On the other hand, there is no present-day biblical commentator who seriously wants to revive the conscious allegorizing interpretation of the parables in all its unrestrained diversity. It is therefore a question of finding the right middle way between two extremes: on the one hand, an arbitrary reading into the parables of edifying thoughts or theological systems and, on the other, a simplifying which cuts out overtones and niceties in the symbolism and thus also—and this may justifiably be said of Jeremias's interpretation of the parables—constricts the message of the parables. The task is thus to find out what may be called "legitimate allegory" and to determine its function in the New Testament parables. Legitimate allegory may most simply be defined so as to include a metaphorical or allegorical use of pictures and symbols for which a similar use may be held to have existed already in the milieu in which Jesus appeared, that is, to the extent that it can be supported by Old Testament or Jewish texts. For insofar as the allegorizing of a definite motif was already traditional in Judaism, there is from the point of view of principle nothing to hinder Jesus from also having used this form of expression.

In connection with a consideration of this sort, it is not out of the way to pay attention to the words of Jesus quoted together with the parable of the sower. To the disciples' question about the contents of the parable Jesus answers: "To you has been given the secret (μυστήριον) of the kingdom of God" (Mark 4:11 and parallels). This saying, as is known, is placed in contrast to the assertion that those who stand outside only understand that it is a question of parables (for them "everything is in parables") the contents of which are difficult to comprehend. Many commentators hold this logion to be a secondary expansion of the original tradition, an attempt on the part of the early church to come to terms partly with the problem of the parables and partly with the so-called messianic secret. It would take us too far afield here to go into the problems which are linked with the passage's quotation from Isaiah about seeing and hearing but yet not understanding (Isa. 6:9 f.). It is here sufficient to bear in mind the conception of *mystērion* and ask if it is even likely that the early church should have considered the problem of the parables as complicated and "secret," while the matter for Jesus himself was simple and easily understood. Is it not, in actual fact, the romantic conception about "the simple teaching of Jesus" which dominates such an assumption?

That the idea *mystērion* already in pre-Christian times occupied a prominent place in the eschatological thinking of the Jewish milieu has been revealed by the Qumran texts and their use of the term *raz*. But quite independent of these texts and before their discovery, a Swedish exegete, Nils Johansson, showed in an article, which has unfortunately never been translated into any of the internationally current languages, that "the secret" in an organic way refers to Jesus' messianic consciousness and to the entirety of his mission, the most important point of which during the days of his preaching and teaching still lay in the future but nevertheless already marked the contents of his preaching and teaching. The secret which is on the way to being revealed is the death and resurrection of the Son of man.[13] It is first, in the light of these events, that the figurative speech of the parables becomes really understandable. But even before the course of events cast the final light over what Jesus had earlier said and thus revealed the true interpretation, the disciples were taught by their Master what was the impending task of the Son of man.[14] The "secret" is thus very closely connected with what nowadays in New Testament study is again given a legitimate place in the genuine teaching of Jesus, namely, the certainty that the Son of man must suffer and die in order to be glorified. The combination of the logion about the *mystērion* of the words of the parables with the parable of the sower may naturally be secondary, but the actual words to the disciples about the connection between the message of the parables and the Son of man's own mission bear the mark of originality and genuineness.

If we then go further in the context, we come to the interpretation of the parable of the sower put into the mouth of Jesus (Mark 4:13–20 and parallels). This interpretation is similarly considered by numerous exegetes to be secondary and thus not to have originated with Jesus himself. The reasons for this suspicion are usually twofold.[15] First, in this passage may be found words and turns of phrase which reappear in the New Testament Epistles, and it then is easy to presume that the circumstances of the early church have influenced the formation of the pericope. Secondly, the interpretation has a different point from the actual parable. For while the parable, with its symbolism,

---

[13] Nils Johansson, "Τὸ μυστήριον τῆς βασιλείας τοῦ θεοῦ," *Svensk Teologisk Kvartalskrift* 16 (1940): 3–38; cf. "Gudsrikets hemlighet," in my *Bibelns värld och vår* (1949), pp. 35–63.

[14] See, e.g., Fuller, *Mission and Achievement of Jesus,* pp. 50–78.

[15] Jeremias, *Parables of Jesus,* pp. 61 ff.

paints the miraculous coming of God's kingdom, the interpretation deals with the trials of the disciples and implies an exhortation to endurance. What has struck the exegetes and made them suspicious is the fact that one and the same symbolism, namely, sowing and harvest, is applied to different thoughts or sayings. However, if we examine the theme of "the interpretation" as such, namely, the testing of the disciples, in this particular case without distraction, we must see that here we are dealing with a theme which even elsewhere has its given place in the teaching of Jesus. The thoughts go primarily to the words about discipleship and its conditions, words which in the synoptic tradition have their place in connection with the account of the acknowledgment of the Messiah at Caesarea Philippi (Mark 8:34 ff. and parallels). What is said in "the interpretation" of the parable of the sower thus in itself cannot be widely separated from the words of Jesus about cross bearing or about the denial of one's own claims on life. The first of the above-mentioned reasons for suspicion of the pericope in question is not particularly cogent either. The agreement in terminology between the words of Jesus about discipleship and analogous sayings in the Epistles cannot only depend on the early church having created similar sayings of Jesus, but may even be a consequence of the words and choice of pictures of Jesus having set their stamp on the language used by the first Christian generations. In that respect a basic difference exists between the actual parable as a message of the kingdom of God and "the interpretation" as teaching to the disciples. Provided both are authentic, the former can scarcely have influenced the terminology of the New Testament Epistles to the same extent that the latter must have done. This depends simply on the nature of the subject and its appropriateness for the teaching of the church.

Identical is the case of the parable of the tares in the field (Matt. 13:24–30) and its interpretation (13:36–43). Here again we meet the symbolism of the field and corn doubly applied, partly to the breaking through and triumph of the kingdom of God, partly to discipleship in imitation of the Son of man, in the struggle against this world and its prince, and in expectation of the last day. In the latter part, the language bears the mark not so much of the Epistles as of the idiom of the first Gospel.[16] But any conclusions regarding the genuineness of the introductory parable and the falseness of the "interpretation" should not be drawn too easily from particular peculiarities in the terminology. These may also be explained without prejudging the question of the dual pericope's genuineness or falseness.

The occurrence of a double application of the symbolism in two pictures characteristic of Jesus—the parable of the sower and the parable of the tares among the wheat—is too striking for the explanation to be that the one use originated with Jesus himself, while the early church is supposed to have created the other. This does not really agree with the already established fact that the duality of the proclamation of God's kingdom and the teaching to the disciples is a typical feature of the ministry of Jesus, such as it is described with historical reliability in the synoptic Gospels. When—in a saying of Jesus or at least in a statement on the part of the early church, which also has its significance—it is now said that there lies a "mystery" in the parables (Mark 4:11 and parallels), it is reasonable to assume that the "depth" of the symbolism is itself something of specific importance for Jesus' pictorial way of presentation. This in turn, as we have seen, is connected with the

[16]Jeremias, *Parables of Jesus*, pp. 64 ff.

fact that the symbolism of the parables and their contents has direct relevance to the actual person of Jesus.

It therefore appears as if certain of the parables have two levels, so to speak. These, however, are not independent of one another but, in fact, belong closely together. The first of these levels has to do with the proclamation of the kingdom of God. Tremendous things are about to happen: men are therefore called to decide where they will stand in the event which has already begun. It is the call brought out in the parables in which Jesus addressed the mass of people in Galilee. This call—by Jesus himself or by later tradition—has been concentrated in the summarizing formula: "The time is fulfilled, and the kingdom of God is at hand; repent, and believe in the gospel" (Mark 1:15 and parallels). The other level which is visible in certain of the parables refers to the teaching which Jesus gave to the closer circle of disciples. In the synoptic Gospels it is largely concentrated in what is done after the confession of the disciples at Caesarea Philippi—a confession which witnesses to insight on the part of those handing on the tradition—in that this teaching assumes the faith of those listening in the one speaking. It is a question of discipleship and its terms; but the actual notion of "discipleship" refers to the person of the one who calls himself the Son of man: "If any man would come after me, let him deny himself and take up his cross and follow me" (Mark 8:34 and parallels). This theme is expressed in an undeniable way in "the interpretations" of the parables of the sower and of the tares among the wheat, where the sower suddenly assumes the features of the Son of man, and where the fate of the seed illustrates discipleship and its hazards. This dual nature in the use of symbolism, parallel with the message and teaching of Jesus, is both too essential and too original to be explained only as an expression of a shifting of interest in the early church.

As it now appears, then, the symbols or pictures in the parables of Jesus and their application are too complicated to be reduced in a simple way to a plain uniformity; still wider contexts come into view which further complicate the things we are engaged in. This is the case, if attention is directed not only to the parables in the synoptic Gospels, but if the use of the figures in the Gospel of John is also taken into account.

As a starting point the Johannine words of Jesus about the grain of wheat may suitably be chosen: "The hour has come for the Son of man to be glorified. Truly, truly, I say to you, unless a grain of wheat falls into the earth and dies, it remains alone; but if it dies, it bears much fruit" (John 12:23 f.). After this saying follow words about imitation and discipleship which in content form a clear parallel to the synoptic teaching of the disciples in connection with the account of the acknowledgment of the Messiah at Caesarea Philippi (Mark 8:34 ff. and parallels). The mark of the synoptic teaching of the disciples in question is, however, that in a uniform synoptic tradition it follows the so-called first prediction of suffering (Mark 8:31 and parallels), that is, the teaching of the Son of man's central task of salvation: to suffer and die to open the way to new life. The same transition from a central saying about the Son of man to the teaching about discipleship which has its marks in self-giving and imitation distinguishes the Johannine pericope. The difference is only that the saying about the Son of man is clothed in the garb of metaphor or symbolism: by the aid of a picture taken from the sphere of the motif of a field of wheat, the task of the Son of man is made more fully clear than is the case in any of the predictions of suffering in the synoptic Gospels. Even the analogy between the lot of the Son of man and of his disciples is clearly expressed, thanks to the fact that the picture of the grain of wheat precedes it.

We are thus faced with the fact that the symbolism of the field of wheat in the Johannine pericope appears in the third application, which differs from the two applications which we have earlier found in the section on the synoptic parables. The symbolism thus has a third level. After the message of the kingdom of God and the teaching of the disciples we have, with the help of the same figure, arrived at the teaching about the Son of man. At the same time, it is inevitable that what we have here called the third level forms the prerequisite for the sayings which are made on the other two levels: without what happens to the Son of man the disciples cannot carry out their task, and the harvest of God's kingdom cannot approach its extraordinary and overwhelming maturity. To the "mystery" of the parables belongs the fact that the summons to the kingdom of God and faith in the good tidings inevitably presuppose what is hinted at anticipatorally in the teaching about the Son of man, and what becomes evident on the cross and through the resurrection. But in addition the summons gets its logical consequence in discipleship and all that it implies. The whole of this complex has shown that it may be expressed by the help of variations of the same symbolism.

From where does the figure come which we find in the Johannine saying about the grain of wheat?[17] It has not yet been possible to show any direct source. The hypothesis that the Greek terminology for the mysteries should have had an influence seems less and less credible, especially since the Qumran manuscripts now bring decisive proof

[17]On this see esp., Å. V. Ström, *Vetekornet* (Uppsala: 1944), pp. 416–23, and more recently A. Rasco, "Christus granum frumenti" (Jo. 12, 24), *Verbum Domini* 37 (1959): 12–25, 65–77.

of the thesis that the background of the Fourth Gospel is Jewish and not Hellenistic (at least not directly so). For various reasons it is probable that the presupposition of the motif of the grain of wheat is to be found in the Old Testament or Jewish tradition. The picture of the harvest as a symbol of the judgment is found in the books of the prophets (e.g., Isa. 41:15 f.; Jer. 51:33; Joel 4:13; Amos 9:9).[18] The connection between the figure of the grain of wheat and the resurrection is to be found in rabbinic literature.[19] To this is added a third ingredient—in no way unessential to the messianic ideology: Israel is regarded as the good wheat.[20] The starting points are unquestionably to be found in the Old Testament and in Judaism. Is it, then, the tradition behind the Gospel of John which has created the saying about the grain of wheat as a complement to the synoptic parables containing the motif of the sower and to the synoptic sayings about the Son of man? Again the answer must be that the saying about the grain of wheat in the form of symbolism and in its obvious relation to the teaching of Jesus, as it appears in the synoptic Gospels, is much too essential and original to be able to be assigned to an anonymous transmitter of tradition. The application on three levels of one and the same figure presents itself as a conscious creation and can scarcely have come about by chance. This means that there is reason to think that it originates with Jesus himself.

After the preceding argument it might appear as if the threefold application of a figure would appear only once, since we only lingered over the sower and grain of wheat motif. In actual fact the same phenomenon reappears in connection with other figures.

[18]Cf. the message of John the Baptist, Matt. 3:7–10 and parallel.
[19]bSanh. 90 b. See W. D. Davies, *Paul and Rabbinic Judaism* (New York: Harper & Row, 1965 [paperback]).
[20]CantR. 7:3 § 3.

The kingdom of God is presented in the picture of a candle which is lit and put into a candlestick so that it is visible to all around just as, with another picture, the town on the hill, Jerusalem on Zion, appears as a mark and a sign (Mark 4:21 and parallel; cf. Matt. 5:14 and parallel). In the teaching concerning the disciples the motif varies to the extent that the disciples are represented as the light of the world (Matt. 5:14). Their task is therefore characterized in the following way: "Let your light so shine before men, that they may see your good works and give glory to your Father who is in heaven" (Matt. 5:16). The motif is varied eschatologically to the extent that the disciples must have their loins girded and their lamps burning (Luke 12:35 ff.; Matt. 25:1 ff.). But the light of the kingdom of God cannot be lit and spread abroad and the disciples cannot fulfill their function as lights in the world unless the Messiah by his personal contribution creates the possibilities for this. This is the presupposition which, unexpressed but inevitably, already lies behind the synoptic sayings about the kingdom of God. In the Fourth Gospel, however, we find the christological application of the motif of light in open and unequivocal words: "I am the light of the world; he who follows me will not walk in darkness, but will have the light of life" (John 8:12). As distinct from the saying about the grain of wheat, we here stand before one of the sayings in the first person, which in its form of revelation also witnesses to the self-consciousness of the speaker. It is not a question of a light among others (naturally, neither is it a question of a grain of wheat among other similar ones in the figures dealt with earlier), but here the claim is raised, which is logically contradictory, that what actually is not light, but only presented under the metaphor "light," surpasses all other light. This is what lies in the saying about "the light of the world." Here lie the connecting links with Pauline thought about the relation between Christology and creation (e.g., Col. 1:15 ff.).

There is further material to advance. The ancient figure of the tree of life, in the Old Testament applied to Israel (and its king) or the enemy (e.g., Isa. 11:1 ff.; Ezek. 31:1 ff.; Dan. 4:7), is taken up in the message of Jesus as a symbol of the kingdom of God.[21] We find it above all in the paradoxical parable of the grain of mustard which grows up into a mighty tree (Mark 4:30 ff. and parallels; note especially the play on the wording in Dan. 4:21). A related figure, similarly with roots in the Old Testament conception of the world, is that of the vineyard (Mark 12:1 ff. and parallels). Another level in the use of symbolism, however, appears in the logion about the sound tree which bears good fruit, while the rotten—or dry—tree which bears evil fruit faces destruction (Matt. 7:16–21 and parallels). Even if in this logion the disciples are not directly addressed, however, it appears from its position in various parts of the synoptic Gospels that it has been clearly understood as teaching to the disciples.[22] The christological application is again met in the Gospel of John, which has the saying about the vine in the first person. "I am the true vine" (15:1) and "I am the vine, you are the branches" (15:5). Characteristic even here is the fact that the christological saying is regarded as the presupposition for what is said about discipleship: "He who abides in me, and I in him, he it is that bears much fruit, for apart from me you can do nothing" (15:5). Here again the logical consequence of the application of the symbolism cannot depend on chance, even if it extends over both the synoptic and the Fourth Gospels.

[21] I. Engnell, "Livets träd," *Svensk Bibliskt Uppslagsbok*, part 2, cols. 107–11.

[22] To this may be compared the use of the verb Χαρπιζειν in the Pauline letters.

Quite different is the use of symbolism in the question of the motif of the shepherd. The synoptic form of this motif has already been dealt with above. However, it can now be shown that the Gospel of John openly supplies the key, so to speak, which must be used if one wants to understand the symbolism of the synoptic parable (Luke 15:4–7 and parallel) and the use of the metaphor of the shepherd in general (e.g., Mark 6:34). Again on this occasion it is done in the form of the first person: "I am the good shepherd. The good shepherd lays down his life for the sheep" (John 10:11). Here it is clearly stated that Jesus does not act as ordinary shepherds, and similarly is the shepherd above all others, the "good" shepherd.

Analogous is the case with the motif of the gate as well as the way. In the synoptic tradition these figures characterize the kingdom of God and its coming: "Enter by the narrow gate; . . . for the gate is narrow and the way is hard, that leads to life" (Matt. 7:13 f. and parallel). In the Gospel of John, on the other hand, it is Jesus himself who describes his person and his saving deed in the same figure: "I am the door; if any one enters by me, he will be saved" (10:9), and: "I am the way, and the truth, and the life" (14:6), which—somewhat simplified—means: the true way to life. Even here the fact is that the Johannine formulations openly express the messianic or christological prerequisites which lie unexpressed beneath the synoptic use of the pictures.[23]

Here and there in our generation there have been noted the points of contact and the connection between the parables of the Gospels, on the one hand, and the symbolic deeds and miracles of Jesus, on the other. However, these questions have not as yet been made the subject of more

[23]Above all Hoskyns and Davey, *Riddle of the New Testament,* pp. 116–45 (see also Jeremias, *Parables of Jesus,* pp. 192 f.).

detailed investigation. The existence of cross connections, however, becomes clear not least in an analysis of motifs. The miracle of the feeding of the five thousand, when the crowds were fed with bread the abundance of which is stressed by the fragments gathered up in the baskets, stands out as a link in the message of Jesus about the kingdom of God. The associations with the miracle of the manna (Exod. 16:14 ff.) are intended to lead our thoughts to the idea of the time of salvation (Mark 6:35–44 and parallels; 8:1–10 and parallel). It is also likely that the account of the picking of the ears of corn on the Sabbath (Mark 2:23–28 and parallels) in actual fact brings us face to face with a symbolic act intended to hint at the unlimited richness and fullness of the time of salvation, the freedom to eat of the bread of life.[24] In connection with the account of the miracle of the feeding of the five thousand (John 6:1–13), the Fourth Gospel allows Jesus to take up the symbolism of the bread of life in the speech that follows (6:32–59). The accentuation resides in the fact that this symbolism, the eschatological content of which is actualized for the Jews by the ritual of the Passover,[25] is applied in the Johannine words of Jesus to the actual person of Jesus, again in a first person expression: "I am the bread of life" (John 6:48).

It appears likely that the Fourth Gospel, in this characteristically christological use of the figure of parables and symbolic deeds, reveals a feature which is worth noticing. The question arises whether this feature is the result of a development which has taken place in the Johannine tradition and thus has its origin in its transmitter. Against such an assumption, however, is the fact that the basic forms of the parables, that is, the figures applied to the kingdom of

---

[24]On this subject see H. Riesenfeld, *Jésus transfiguré* (1947), pp. 318–30.

[25]B. Gärtner, *John 6* (Coni. Neotest., 17; Uppsala, 1959).

God, are not found at all in connection with the tradition of the Fourth Gospel but in the synoptic traditions which differ from it. A secondary development would, on the other hand, presuppose that the basic material was available. It therefore looks as if the Gospel of John has preserved an original feature, belonging to the teaching of Jesus himself within the circle of the disciples. As has already been pointed out above, the teaching of the person and the task of the Son of man take up a central position in the ministry of Jesus, as it is reported in the synoptic Gospels. As we have likewise seen, it is not only that the characteristic circumstances for the dawning of the kingdom of God, described in the parable of the lost sheep, assume by implication that the seeking shepherd is a reality, but further the actual synoptic version shows that Jesus stands out as the awaited messianic "shepherd" who takes an interest in the abandoned people, which is the case, for instance, in the description of the feeding of the five thousand (Mark 6:32–44 and parallels).

Further, however, there lies a decisive indication in the fact that actually even in the synoptic tradition there are two contexts in which the figure of the type in question is expressly applied to the person of Jesus. In one of these contexts there does not exist any doubt that this christological application has its origin in Jesus himself. We refer to the Last Supper and the institution of communion, when Jesus, in symbolic form, identified the bread with his person: "Take; this is my body" (τὸ σῶμά μου, Mark 14:22 and parallels). There is no doubt at all that it is here a question of a conscious linking up with the motif of the bread of life and with the symbolism of the meal in association with the message of the kingdom of God during the earlier public ministry of Jesus. At the same time, the intentional concentration of the whole circle of motifs on the person of

Jesus is obvious. This is borne out by the parallel application of the vine motif: "This is my blood" (Mark 14:24 and parallels), which in turn assumes the presence and meaning of the motif, not only in the Old Testament religious tradition, but above all in the message of God's kingdom given by Jesus (Mark 2:22 and parallels; John 2:1–11; cf. John 15:1–6). The other case consists of a christologically interpreted quotation from the Psalms, which forms the conclusion of the parable about the wicked owner of the vineyard: "The very stone which the builders rejected has become the head of the corner" (Mark 12:10 and parallels; quoted from Ps. 117:22 LXX). Whether the connection between the parable and the concluding quotation is original may be called in question: the parable leads forward to the "son's" death, while the quotation aims at illustrating the rehabilitation of "the stone," that is, the Messiah.[26] Extraordinarily strong reasons, however, speak in favor of understanding the quotation, in its messianic reference, as going back to Jesus himself, even if the connection with the parable is secondary. The proof of the genuineness of the quotation as a saying of Jesus seems to lie in the fact that this saying about the rejected and rehabilitated stone takes up a prominent place in early Christian writings outside the Gospel tradition (esp. Acts 4:11 and 1 Pet. 2:7; cf. also the pre-Christian literature).[27] We may thus conclude that Jesus has used the figure of the solid rock or foundation in a parable which belongs most closely to the parables about the kingdom of God (Matt. 7:24 f. and parallel), that the motif recurs in the application to discipleship in the logion where Peter is depicted as the rock

---

[26]J. Schmid, *Das Evangelium nach Markus*[3] (Regensburger N.T.) (1954), pp. 220 f.

[27]V. Taylor, *The Gospel According to St. Mark* (New York: St. Martin's Press, 1952), p. 447, where further references are given; cf. also Cole, *New Temple*.

(Matt. 16:18), and that the figure, in a clearly authentic logion, is finally applied messianically or christologically to Jesus himself (Mark 12:10 and parallels), when all these three characteristic forms—or interpretations—of one and the same figure occur in the synoptic tradition. The phenomenon is much too obvious to depend on a coincidence and much too complete to be explained as a secondary development.

The observations made here, as we have seen, also reveal relations which seem to exist between the synoptic tradition, on the one hand, and the Johannine, on the other. It is in the latter that the christological application of the figure principally occurs, but this coincides with the meaning and the deeper form given in general to the Christology of the Fourth Gospel. The question arises whether the Gospel of John has preserved certain parts of the christological teaching of Jesus which have not gained a footing in the synoptic tradition. This teaching—and this is the case even with parts of the material of the synoptic tradition—had been imparted to the closer circle of the disciples and, therefore, at first had a more esoteric character.

What has been put forward here in the form of a brief survey is intended to show that a more detailed analysis of figures used in our Gospels may, on the one hand, further contribute to the exegesis of the parables and may, on the other, throw further light on the problematic relations between the synoptic and the Johannine traditions.

VIII. Paul's "Grain of Wheat" Analogy and the Argument of 1 Corinthians 15

It has become traditional for expositors of 1 Corinthians 15 to introduce the chapter with the rubric, "the resurrection of the dead"—a practice that has been transmitted from commentary to commentary, as is so often the case.[1] It also is customary to consider the introductory section, the kerygmatic formula cited by Paul (15:3–7), as both the starting point and the focal point of the case which Paul presents and of the train of thought which he develops in the chapter. In this connection, it is well to reflect upon the fact that the person who now reads the New Testament finds himself in a rather different situation from that of the original recipients to whom the apostle first addressed himself. For us, the section which contains the quotation from the proclamation of the resurrection is of utmost significance, since our only knowledge of this nugget comes from this passage. To the Corinthians, however, the kerygma in this form was well-known—as the author of the Epistle clearly attests by his introductory remarks (15:1–3). Why, then, does he in his letter once again expressly and verbally reproduce that which was already familiar? So that he might explicate it in a theological tractate? But the subsequent material deals with the resurrection of Christ only

[1]So, e.g., J. Weiss, *Der erste Korintherbrief* (Kritische-exegetische Kommentar über das NT 5) (10th ed.; Göttingen: 1925); H. Lietzmann, *An die Korinther I-II, 4,* supplemented ed. by W. G. Kümmel (Handbuch zum NT 9; Tübingen: 1949); E. -B. Allo, *Saint Paul: Première épître aux Corinthiens* (Études Bibliques; Paris: 1934); H. D. Wendland, *Die Briefe an die Korinther* (6th ed. NT Deutsch 7; Göttingen: 1954); H. Odeberg, *Korintierbreven* (2nd ed.; Stockholm: 1953); cf. J. Héring, *La première Épître de S. Paul aux Corinthiens* (Commentaire du NT 8; Neuchâtel: 1949).

to a limited degree. Nor could he have done it out of regard for a grateful posterity. The reason for his introducing this citation cannot lie in the general importance of this item of instruction concerning the resurrection of Christ, but must be sought in what follows. The kerygma is inserted not for the purpose of presenting a fundamental point of instruction, but in order to set the stage for discussing an actual problem. In my opinion, it is verse 12 that provides the key to the chapter.

The occasion for Paul's dealing with the themes that permeate chapter 15 has been provided by the Corinthian "pneumatics" or "spiritualists." It still remains an open question whether or to what extent "Gnostics" is the most appropriate designation for these people. Probably their mystic-ecstatic experiences and their assurance that they possessed the Spirit led them to the conclusion that those who truly believe in Christ are already living in "the age to come," having already been resurrected with Christ through baptism and thus having left death behind them (cf. 2 Tim. 2:18).[2] How the representatives of such "pneumaticism" reacted to the continued occurrences of death in the community is not clear from this context. In any event, their belief must have carried along with it a convulsive repugnance for looking the problem of death in the eye. Nor is it clear whether the practice of baptism for the dead, to which Paul later alludes (15:29), was also observed by the false teachers who are being addressed, or whether it has simply been introduced into the train of thought as an independent argument. Nevertheless, in the light of the inconsistency of thought and of conduct which is characteristic of any such "pneumaticism" and which usually becomes apparent precisely in relationship to death, it is

[2]E.g., Wendland, *Die Briefe,* p. 125; Lietzmann, *An die Korinther,* pp. 192, 194.

not inherently impossible that this passage also refers to the same persons who fancy themselves to be exempt from death. As is apparent from the way in which Paul constructs his argument, the actual concern of the entire chapter is the refutation of this false teaching, even though in his polemic against a false view, in typical Pauline fashion, the multitude of inrushing ideas sometimes obscure the original intention and harness the letter's author with respect to the more central questions. It is on this account that the opponents and their delusion about the resurrection tend to vanish more and more from the field of vision.

When seen from this perspective, it follows that the formal citation of the kerygma (15:1–11) simply provides Paul with a starting point from which to base his attack on those members of the Corinthian community who assert that the resurrection of true Christians has already taken place. That constitutes a skillful stratagem on the part of the apostle, for in the acknowledgment of the kerygma, both the false teachers and the author of the Epistle were in agreement. Through a methodical exploiting of this situation, Paul now, in characteristic fashion, carries it through to its logical implications—that the actual death and actual resurrection of Christ also imply death as a presupposition for the actual resurrection of those who believe in Christ. (From our point of view, to be sure, we can agree with Luther that this line of argument scarcely would have convinced the dissenters, and thus that the remarks of the apostle have their real significance as a recital of important items of Christian belief and of Christian hope; but this was far from Paul's concern as he dictated the letter!)[3] From a historical point of view, the aim of the argument in chapter 15 is to refute certain actual Corinthian Christians who did not deny the resurrection as such, but who lived in the

[3]Héring, La première Épître, p. 137.

illusion that their highest earthly state of existence [*Dasein*] already represented the postresurrection state of eternal life.[4]

This concise overview of the assumptions presupposed by the flow of thought in our chapter suffices to make it apparent that the theme of the presentation really should not be formulated with the words, "the resurrection of the dead," but rather, "Death as the presupposition for resurrection." What Paul wants to make clear to the false teachers is not the fact of the resurrection, which was not questioned by any party in the community, but the necessity of physical death as a condition for the possibility of a genuine resurrection.[5] To the very end of the chapter, which in this instance encompasses the complete sequence of ideas, the problem revolves around the necessity of death and around overcoming death—not bypassing death, but going right through it—in relationship to the resurrection, which is, in this case, itself less problematic.

That the above presentation of the problem is both appropriate in terms of the Pauline mode of argument and correct in relation to the text under consideration is in

[4]Verse 19 is of crucial importance for understanding the entire context. Héring correctly points out that, in 15:19, the word "alone" ($\mu\acute{o}\nu o\nu$) refers back to "this" ($\tau\alpha\acute{u}\tau\eta$), and is thus to be taken with the prepositional phrase "in this life" ($\dot{\epsilon}\eta$ $\tau\mathring{\eta}$ $\zeta\omega\mathring{\eta}$ $\tau\alpha\acute{u}\tau\mathring{\eta}$), This expression with its explicit preposition, however, gives rise to further considerations. What is the thrust here of "in" ($\dot{\epsilon}\nu$)? Héring gives the excellent translation "in the limits of this life"(*dans les limites de cette vie*). Thus he has taken into consideration the problem of in what sense the "in" is to be construed (see Walter Bauer, *A Greek-English Lexicon of the NT* . . . , trans. and ed. William F. Arndt and F. Wilbur Gingrich [Chicago: University of Chicago Press, 1957], *sub voce* IV.I). A further question concerns the precise meaning of "this life." I would suggest the paraphrase, "life as it is visibly lived here."

[5]In the kerygmatic formula of 15:3–7, the tradition-bound enumeration of witnesses to the resurrection of Christ misleads one to suppose that the crucial point in Paul's argumentation rests in the fact of the resurrection. But in view of 5:12 ff., this is not the case. Much more important for the development of the argument is the claim that Jesus had died and was buried, for this is the crucial presupposition for his resurrection

no small measure established, in my opinion, by the way in which the apostle has used the "grain of wheat" analogy (15:36–44). That is to say, in terms of both the immediate context and the comments throughout the entire chapter, this analogy occupies a central position.

How, then, is the symbolism of the grain of wheat applied in terms of concepts, and whence did the usage of this imagery originate in the sense in which Paul here employs it? Surprisingly, interpretations of the passage have been little concerned with such questions. Apparently this is because the language of the New Testament writings is so rich in imagery that one simply takes it for granted. Nevertheless, it can immediately be assumed that Paul has not independently created the analogy. The symbolism of sowing and reaping was theologically loaded in the tradition in which Paul stood and occurs both in the Old Testament writings and in rabbinic literature.[6] It must be assumed that a cultured Jew would be acquainted with it. But what is more important to note is that it is just this sort of traditionally given pictorial language that cannot be used as loosely as is possible with imagery created on the spur of the moment. On these grounds it becomes even less likely that Paul has been influenced by the manifold use of wheat symbolism in the Greek cultural tradition. Previous investigations have suggested the conclusion that the Pauline application of the imagery seems to have no Hellenistic roots.

Characteristic of the examples which have been discovered in rabbinic literature is the familiar (alleged) answer of Rabbi Meir to Queen Cleopatra's question as to whether the dead arise naked or clothed: "If a grain of

---

[6]Cf. F. Hauck, θερίζω-θερισμός, in Kittel, vol. 3; H. L. Strack and P. Billerbeck, *Kommentar zum NT aus Talmud und Midrasch* IV.2 (Munich, 1928), Index under "Ernte," "Saat," "Samenkorn"; Lietzmann, *An die Korinther*, pp. 83 f.; Ström, *Vetekornet*, pp. 416–23.

wheat, which is buried naked, comes forth clothed in many garments, how much more so the righteous who are buried in their clothing!" (Bab. Talmud, *Sanhedrin* 90b). By comparison with this example, Paul develops the line of thought in a different direction. What he wants to say is as follows: The body (σῶμα) that comes forth in the resurrection ("grows up," according to the analogy) is something different from the dead earthly body that was buried ("sown") in the earth. Instead, a transformation takes place, and this represents a higher mode of existence. To this extent Paul and Rabbi Meir agree in the way they coin the imagery. The Rabbi, however, is interested in the implication of the metaphor for the *result* of the transformation, which is indicated by Paul through the words "incorruption" (ἀφθαρσία), "glory" (δόξα), and "power" (δύναμις); for the apostle, on the other hand, the point lies in the conditional clause, "unless it dies" (15:36, ἐὰν μὴ ἀποθάνῃ), which plays no direct role in the rabbinic text. Death is the *presupposition* for the transformation, and thus the dying of the grain of wheat has become the central point of the analogy for Paul.[7] The remarks that follow (15:37–44) are also governed by the same presupposition—the transformation which takes place in the resurrection is so radical that without a radical death it is inconceivable and impossible. It becomes apparent here that the *tertium comparationis* [linking concept] for relating the christological kerygma to the eschatological lot of the individual Christian is much more the idea of death than it is that of resurrection.

Is it possible, then, that Paul is the author of the very familiar and highly significant *modification* of the symbolism of sowing and harvesting which is introduced here? It is

---

[7]Lietzmann, *An die Korinther*, p. 83: "By the simile of the seed-grain he first (15:36) illustrates the necessity of death (as in John 12:24), then (15:37–38) the event of being clothed with the new resurrection body."

well-known that a similar use of the imagery occurs else-where in the New Testament, in John 12:24: "Unless the grain of wheat dies when it falls into the ground, it re-mains by itself; but if it dies, it produces much fruit" (ἐὰν μὴ ὁ κόκκος τοῦ σίτου πεσὼν εἰς τὴν γῆν ἀποθάνῃ, αὐτὸς μόνος μένει. ἐὰν δὲ ἀποθάνῃ πολὺν καρπὸν φέρει). The fact that Paul and John agree in the subordinate clause "unless it dies" (ἐὰν μὴ ἀποθάνῃ), which is central to both texts, is in any event strik-ing. Could it be that there is dependence of one on the other? Two factors seem to militate against that suggestion. First of all, one is not inclined, a priori, to think that there is any direct relationship between Paul and the Fourth Gospel.[8] Secondly, it should be noted that the analogy is applied in a christological setting in John; the grain of wheat that dies and lives again signifies the messianic death and resurrec-tion of Jesus. For Paul, however, the imagery occurs in an anthropological context and has to do with the lot of the individual Christian—that is, with his death and his resurrection.

On closer examination, however, it appears that the rela-tionships are much more complicated than to be susceptible to such a simple analysis. On the basis of the remaining instances in which Paul employs the imagery of sowing (and, when the occasion arises, also of harvesting), it ap-pears that the symbolism is not only used in a strictly pictorial manner, but that a metaphorical use also is pre-supposed (Gal. 6:8; 1 Cor. 9:11; 2 Cor. 9:6–10).[9] Without any further explanation, the terminology of sowing and harvesting is used in such a way as to signify active par-ticipation in the Christian life and the result of such partici-

---

[8]Allo, St. Paul, p. 421, suggests the possibility that Paul himself refers to a saying of Jesus that is only preserved for us in the Johannine tradi-tion. Ström, Vetekornet, pp. 418 f., debates whether the Fourth Gospel could be dependent on Paul, but dismisses this hypothesis as improbable.
[9]Cf. chap. 9, below.

pation. Indeed, this means that Paul was able to count on the fact that the metaphorical use was familiar to his recipients, for every metaphorical expression presupposes a common understanding of its thrust on the part of both speaker and listener, writer and reader. But whence did the Christians in Galatia or Corinth derive an awareness of such nuances of the expression? Apparently from the instruction they had received, from catechesis. It is strange that in the most frequently used modern commentaries, none of the commentators has noted that 1 Corinthians 9:11 presents a play on words based on a catechetical theme. It is only possible to understand that kind of language—"If we have sown what is pneumatic in you, is it a great matter if we harvest from you what is sarkic?" (εἰ ἡμεῖς ὑμῖν τὰ πνευματικὰ ἐσπείραμεν, μέγα εἰ ἡμεῖς ὑμῶν τὰ σαρκικὰ θερίσομεν)—if we presuppose that the Corinthians had previously heard about sowing in the flesh and reaping in the spirit—and that Paul was aware of this fact. In all probability, 1 Peter 1:23 also reflects a similarly catechetical situation: "Having been begotten anew, not of corruptible but of incorruptible seed, by means of the living and abiding word of God" (ἀναγεγεννημένοι οὐκ ἐκ σπορᾶς φθαρτῆς ἀλλὰ ἀφθάρτου διὰ λόγου ζῶντος θεοῦ καὶ μένοντος). Now the contrasting couplet, corruptible/incorruptible, used in connection with the imagery of sowing, quite clearly recalls the formulation in our Pauline passage—"it is sown in corruption, it is raised in incorruption" (1 Cor. 15:42, σπείρεται ἐν φθορᾷ ἐγείρεται ἐν ἀφθαρσίᾳ)—and also the words of Galatians 6:8—"He who sows (anything) into his own flesh will reap corruption from the flesh" (ὁ σπείρων εἰς τὴν σάρκα ἑαυτοῦ ἐκ τῆς σαρκὸς θερίσει φθοράν).

Now it might seem as though the examples cited are much too different to be able to be derived from a common denominator. As we already have noted, the imagery of sowing is used or interpreted somewhat differently in the passages cited above from Paul and 1 Peter. Sometimes it refers to the kind of Christian existence that issues from the sowing (1 Pet. 1:23), sometimes it designates the activity of the apostle (1 Cor. 9:11) or of believers (2 Cor. 9:10; Gal. 6:8), and sometimes the eschatological transformation of individual Christians (1 Cor. 15:36 ff.). Is it possible to conclude that we have here anything other than a multicolored and unrelated variety in the use of a familiar image?

An investigation of the pictorial language found in the Gospels, and especially in the parables of Jesus, however, suggests that characteristic variations occur in the use of imagery throughout a series of figurative motifs. The situation encountered here is closely related to that which has also been studied, although in a somewhat different context, by modern philosophy of religion.[10] By investigating religious symbolic language, a phenomenon has been isolated which is called the "multivalence" of religious symbols. It is not difficult to illustrate the appearance of such a situation in the New Testament material. For example, the imagery of light in the words attributed to Jesus in the Gospels has a threefold significance: the kingdom of God, with reference to its coming (Mark 4:21); the task of the disciples, both their activity as actual followers of Jesus and (as seen from the perspective of the later community) the Christian life in general (Matt. 5:14, 16); and, finally, the messianic person and work of Jesus (John 8:12). The same can be said for the imagery of the tree (for which, it should be noted, the age-old symbolism of the tree of life is basic): the kingdom of heaven is the universal tree that grows up from a tiny mustard seed (Mark 4:30 ff. and

---

[10]See, e.g., M. Eliade, "Methodological Remarks on the Study of Religious Symbolism," in *The History of Religions*, ed. M. Eliade and J. M. Kitagawa (Chicago: University of Chicago Press, 1959), pp. 86–107.

parallels); the disciples ought to become like trees that bear good fruits (Matt. 7:16–21 and parallel); finally, Jesus as Messiah is the vine (John 15:1) on which the disciples are to be fruit-bearing branches (John 15:5). This phenomenon, which can be illustrated by a number of other images, occurs in the Gospels in such a way that the christological use of the symbolism usually is limited to the Fourth Gospel —a fact that is in harmony with the christological orientation of that writing. Nevertheless, what is of primary significance is that clear traces of this special use of symbolism also can be seen in the Synoptics.[11]

Such observations entitle us to conclude that the imagery of sowing, insofar as it has to do with the mission and activity of the apostle (1 Cor. 9:11) or of the community and its members (2 Cor. 9:10; Gal. 6:8), stands in a tradition that was typical for primitive Christian proclamation. This inference is confirmed by a glance at the second part of the so-called parable of the soil (or, of the sower) in the Synoptics (Mark 4:14–20 and parallels), where the actual parable (Mark 4:3–8 and parallels), which has to do with the coming of the kingdom of God, is interpreted in such a way that the conditions for discipleship emerge as the theme. Quite apart from the question of to what extent this "interpretation" is authentic or secondary, its significance for our discussion lies in the fact that its theme is more closely related to primitive Christian catechesis, which was directly concerned with the life of Christians, than is the actual parable itself. A synoptic comparison of the parallels to Mark 4:14–20 thus can provide positive information concerning the emergence of the metaphors used in catechesis as they are connected to the imagery of sowing and reaping (or of bearing fruit). Finally, the problem of the christological interpretation of the grain of wheat imagery in

[11]Cf. chap. 7, above.

Paul's "Grain of Wheat" Analogy

John 12:24 must be mentioned once again. It is striking that a saying of Jesus concerning following him, which speaks about losing and preserving life (John 12:25 f.), is attached to this logion. In terms of content, the passage in John 12:24–26 corresponds exactly to the synoptic sayings that follow the narrative about the recognition of Jesus' messiahship at Caesarea Philippi—that is, to the first passion prediction and to the statements about following Jesus and about discipleship (Mark 8:31, 34 f. and parallels). In any event, from the fact that both in the synoptic tradition and also in the Fourth Gospel the role of the Son of man in dying and rising is linked with the lot of the disciples in renouncing all to follow Jesus, it follows that the parallelism between the aspect of suffering referred to in the Christology and that mentioned in statements about discipleship has been anchored firmly in the primitive Christian tradition.

The hypothesis suggested above—that in all probability, pictorial motifs in Paul may have derived from a general catechetical situation[12]—finds further support in the fact that another analogy, which also is found in the Gospels, occurs (like the imagery of sowing) partly in the Pauline letters and partly in a clearly catechetical setting in passages outside the Pauline corpus. I refer to the symbolism of the temple, which, in an extended sense, is used of the body.[13] In the Gospels—and not only in the Fourth Gospel—it

[12]Cf. C. F. D. Moule, *The Epistles to the Colossians and Philemon* (Cambridge: Cambridge University Press, 1957), pp. 50 f., and "The Use of Parables and Sayings as Illustration Material in Early Christian Catechism," *Journal of Theological Studies* 3 (1952): 75–79; also Selwyn, *First Epistle of St. Peter.*

[13]Selwyn, *First Epistle of St. Peter*, pp. 285–91; M. Simon, "Retour du Christ et reconstruction du Temple dans la pensée chrétienne primitive," *Aux sources de la tradition chrétienne* (Mélanges M. Goguel; Neuchâtel: 1950), pp. 247–57; C. F. D. Moule, "Sanctuary and Sacrifice in the Church of the New Testament," *Journal of Theological Studies* 1 (1950): 29–41; Cole, *New Temple*; J. Dupont, Σὺν Χριστῷ: *l'union avec le Christ suivant saint Paul* (Bruges/Louvain/Paris: 1952), 1: 146–50.

characteristically appears in a christological pronouncement, and that in an adaptation of a saying which, in essentials, probably goes back to Jesus himself. Thus the following words are attributed to the false witnesses at the trial: "We have heard that he said, 'I will destroy this Temple made with hands and in three days build another not made with hands'" (Mark 14:58 and parallel, cf. John 2:19–21). Paul, who calls Christians "God's temple" (1 Cor. 3:16 ff., ναὸς θεοῦ) and calls their body "a temple of the holy spirit in you" (1 Cor. 6:19, ναὸς τοῦ ἐν ὑμῖν ἁγίου πνεύματος), uses the temple or house symbolism in an anthropological-eschatological manner in the difficult passage in 2 Corinthians 5:1–10.[14] It is striking that the "house in the heavens" (οἰκία ἐν τοῖς οὐρανοῖς) is described as "made without hands" (ἀχειροποίητος) and "eternal" (2 Cor. 5:1, αἰώνιος), which provides a direct counterpart to the second member of the contrasting pair employed in 1 Corinthians 15:42—corruptible (φθαρτός)/incorruptible (ἄφθαρτος).[15]

A question that was posed above has yet to be answered, namely, is there any kind of dependence, in any direction, between the Johannine saying about the grain of wheat (John 12:24) and the Pauline statement about sowing grain (1 Cor. 15:36 ff.)? It is my contention that this question can be answered in the affirmative. The foregoing in-

---

[14]In addition to the commentaries, this passage is treated in detail by Rudolf Bultmann, *Exegetische Probleme des zweiten Korintherbriefes* (Symb. Bibl. Upsal. 9; Upsala: 1947), pp. 3–12; J. Dupont, Σὺν Χριστῷ, pp. 135–91; R. De Langhe, "Judaïsme ou hellénisme en rapport avec le Nouveau Testament," *L'attente du Messie* (Mélanges J. Coppens, Recherches bibliques: Bruges/Paris: 1954), pp. 179–81; J. N. Sevenester, "Einige Bemerkungen über den 'Zwischenzustand' bei Paulus," *New Testament Studies* (1954/55), 1: 291–96; A. Feuillet, "Mort du Christ et mort du chrétien d'après les épîtres pauliniennes," *Revue Biblique* 66 (1959): 481–513.

[15]On the correlative terms "made with hands," χειροποίητος/"not made with hands" (ἀχειροποίητος), which obviously relate to a catechetical tradition, see Moule, "Sanctuary and Sacrifice," pp. 33 f.

vestigation has demonstrated that the metaphorical use of the imagery of sowing, with reference to the life and activity of the disciples as well as of Christians, occurs both in the Gospels and in primitive Christian parenesis as it comes to light in the Pauline letters and in 1 Peter. Other pictorial motifs are used in a similar manner. Conversely, it is unlikely that such a figurative motif would be coined for anthropological-eschatological purposes, thus being applied to the death and new life of the individual Christian, as is the case with the Pauline saying about the grain of wheat. The sole parallel to this situation is the Pauline application of the temple or house imagery to death and the resurrection body in 2 Corinthians 5:1 ff.[16] In the latter case, it can be argued that a christological saying of Jesus, which still retains its original features in the Gospel tradition, has been modified in such a manner that it depicts the way in which the individual Christian follows Jesus through death to resurrection, just as for Christ the destruction of the earthly body was the presupposition for resurrection and glorification. Correspondingly, the Pauline statement about the grain of wheat gives expression to a thought that is similar in content. Moreover, in both instances it is evident that the christological interpretation of the imagery is primary in comparison to the anthropological-eschatological, just as the thought of "following" Jesus has as its presupposition the path of suffering traveled by the Son of man. Accordingly, the Pauline presentation of the imagery of sowing probably consists of an adaptation of the christological symbolism of the grain of wheat into a statement about follow-

---

[16]Contrary to John A. T. Robinson, *The Body: A Study in Pauline Theology* (Studies in Biblical Theology 5; London: SCM Press, 1952), pp. 75–79, and Feuillet, "Mort du Christ," pp. 498 f., I agree with the majority of commentators that the imagery refers to the resurrection body of the individual Christian and not to a collective entity or to the heavenly Christ.

ing Jesus and, in addition, of an eschatological sharpening of this statement with reference to the death and resurrection of the individual Christian. Obviously, a development has taken place here that can be explained most easily if one assumes that older material has provided the point of departure in John 12:24–26. This adaptation of the symbolism may very well have been the work of Paul himself, as also seems to be the case with reference to the temple imagery. Thus it is probable that the tradition about a saying of Jesus (originally homogeneous or compound), which first comes to our attention in John 12:24–26, was known already in Paul's day in basically the same form; and for his part, Paul has completed the transference of the pictorial motif from the first to the second part of this saying of Jesus.[17]

This complicated situation, which is typical of the mode of expression found in the New Testament, whereby multivalence and inner homogeneity of symbolism do not neutralize one another is most forcefully illustrated in 1 Clement 24:5. Indeed, it cannot be doubted that this chapter of 1 Clement contains clear allusions to 1 Corinthians 15.[18] The analogy about sowing wheat is used, just as in 1 Corinthians 15:36 ff., in an anthropological-eschatological sense. At the same time, however, the wording used in the passage from 1 Clement furnishes additional clues. On the one hand, there are obvious connections with the synoptic imagery of the parable of the soil (or sower) and its interpretation (Mark 4:3–8, 14–20, and parallels): "The sower went out and cast each of his seeds into the ground.

---

[17]The Johannine word "alone" ($\mu\acute{o}\nu o\varsigma$) is paralleled by the Pauline "naked" ($\gamma\upsilon\mu\nu\acute{o}\varsigma$, 1 Cor. 15:37). The idea of nakedness, which also occurs in the Jewish imagery of the grain of wheat referred to earlier, already in Paul's day may have been linked to this analogy in Jewish circles.

[18]See The Oxford Society of Historical Theology, *The New Testament in the Apostolic Fathers* (London: Oxford University Press, 1905), 41 f.

. . . From a single seed it increases manifold and produces fruit" (ἐξῆλθεν ὁ σπείρων καὶ ἔβαλεν εἰς τὴν γῆν ἕκαστον τῶν σπερμάτων . . . ἐκ τοῦ ἑνὸς πλείονα αὔξει καὶ ἐκφέρει καρπόν). On the other hand the conclusion is irresistible that the formulation in 1 Clement 24:5 goes even beyond 1 Corinthians 15:36 ff. and has been assimilated to John 12:24: "which, withered and naked, decay when they fall into the ground" (ἅτινα πεσόντα εἰς τὴν γῆν ξηρὰ καὶ γυμνὰ διαλύεται.[19] Here, then, the entire range of associations is explored.[20] It follows that, although the interpretation of a pictorial motif may branch out in various directions, the basic unity of the various interpretations is preserved through the all-embracing homogeneity of the symbolism. This observation is in accord with the state of affairs that obtains for religious pictorial language in general.

There remains to be noticed a skillful adaptation of the grain of wheat imagery in the letters of Ignatius of Antioch: "I am God's wheat, and I am being ground by beast's teeth" (Rom. 4:1, σῖτός εἰμι θεοῦ καὶ δι' ὀδόντων θηρίων ἀλήθομαι). The necessary path through death to new life is not illustrated here by using the imagery of how the grain of wheat is transformed in the ground, but by means of one aspect of the process whereby grain is transformed into bread, the grinding of the corn. Thus both John 12:34 (σῖτος) and 1 Corinthians 15:36 ff., with its anthropological-eschatological use of the figure, are presupposed by the language used in Ignatius and cannot be overlooked. It is not conceivable that Ignatius is to be credited with the miracle of having freely created this expression.

[19]The opposing ideas of "decaying" (διαλύειν [διάλυσις]) and "raising up" (ἀνιστάναι) are reminiscent of Mark 14:58 according to D, it: "I will destroy this Temple . . . and in three days I will raise up another not made with hands" (ἐγὸ καταλύσω τὸν ναὸν τοῦτον . . . καὶ διὰ τριῶν ἡμερῶν ἄλλον ἀναστήσω ἀχειροποίητον).

[20]The wooden methodology of H. Köster, Synoptische Überlieferung bei den apostolischen Vätern (Texte und Uutersuchungen 65; Berlin: 1957), which does not pay close attention to the nature of religious language and religious thinking, is impotent to track down such allusions and suggestions.

Finally, by way of conclusion, it may be suggested that our analysis of the grain of wheat analogy also provides a contribution to the understanding of the development through which Pauline thinking about death had passed. In 1 Thessalonians, Paul is entirely concerned with the expectation of the parousia (1 Thess. 4:15–17). Even though he is also conscious of the fact that Christians have died and will continue to die (4:16), death does not seem to be a personal problem for him. First Corinthians marks a new stage of development in this respect. The confrontation with the "pneumatics" has given the apostle the occasion to emphasize the necessity of death.[21] At the same time, the inference drawn from Jesus' route through death to the disciples' route through death (cf. John 12:24–26) is introduced as a point of polemic against the false teachers. The concluding section of chapter 15, however, indicates that Paul also feels himself to be personally involved in the question of death (15:53–57). In 2 Corinthians, he now soberly reckons not only with the possibility, but with the necessity of his own death (5:1–10). The present reality of suffering not only becomes a test of patience, but a confrontation with the seriousness of death (e.g., 2 Cor. 1:5, 4:16, 7:4). Finally, in Philippians, the apostle has fought his way through to clarity of thought and to a deeper confidence (e.g., 1:19–24).[22] The path of following Jesus leads down to death. But precisely because it has to do with *following* Jesus, it opens the door to that which "follows."

---

[21]In view of the caustic precision employed in the argument of 1 Cor. 15 and 2 Cor. 5, it is not very likely that Paul has misunderstood his opponents (as Bultmann, *Exegetische*, p. 4, claimed).

[22]Cf. also Rom. 6:1–11 and 8:12–23, 31–39, and see the comments on these passages by O. Kuss, *Der Römerbrief*, fascicle 1 (Regensburg: 1957), pp. 255–60; in addition, Feuillet, "Mort du Christ."

IX. Parabolic Language in the Pauline Epistles

The literary style of the Pauline Epistles has been the object of many disparate observations rather than of systematic research. The well-known monograph of Bultmann,[1] which appeared many years ago, has not yet been replaced, although the time seems ripe for research proceeding from new starting points and for conclusions resting on wider bases. As a result of a lack of coordination and of rationalization in the scientific work, the Pauline constructions using a genitive have been studied in a detailed manner, while much more important problems of syntax and stylistics in general still await the day when they will be submitted to a thorough examination.[2]

The parabolic language of Paul has been studied in various works which I propose to supplement at some points. I have no intention of devoting time to the collection of metaphors and parables which are found in rich variety in the Pauline *corpus*. Almost all the material in question has been collected together in a very useful way in the works of Heylen and Straub,[3] who, however, have not shown much literary or theological precision. It goes without saying that an examination of the parabolic language may be pursued in

[1]R. Bultmann, *Der Stil der paulinischen Predigt und die kynischstoische Diatribe* (1910).

[2]O. Schmitz, *Die Christus-Gemeinschaft des Paulus im Lichte seines Genetiv-gebrauchs* (1924); cf. further A. Deissmann, *Paulus* (1911; 2nd ed., 1925); E. Norden, *Agnostos Theos* (1913; 2nd ed., 1929); G. Thörnell, *Pastoralbrevens äkthet* (1931); O. Roller, *Das Formular der paulinischen Briefe* (1933).

[3]V. Heylen, "Les métaphores et les métonymies dans les épîtres pauliniennes," *Eph. Theol. Lov.*, 12 (1935): 253–90; W. Straub, *Die Bildersprache des Apostels Paulus* (1937); cf. further, E. Eidem, *Pauli bildvärld* (1913).

different directions. On the one hand, it is possible to give an opinion on the literary qualities of the Epistles, and, on the other, the distinctive features of the psychological constitution of an author reveal themselves in his way of making use of metaphors. These, too, give us a clue to our knowledge of the writer's education and of his contacts with the general civilization of his time and milieu. To give a few examples, it is here that the pictures drawn from games of sport, so popular in the Greek world, from military service, or from law (to the extent to which recourse was had to it in daily life) become relevant.

Now the object of our study is much more restricted. We have limited ourselves to the question of finding out if Paul, who has evidently made use of a fairly large number of pictures and metaphors, has been influenced by the symbolic themes of the parables which constituted an essential part of the teaching of Christ. To the extent that Paul knew the tradition of the sayings of Jesus which must have been living in the church, he was doubtless familiar with the principal parables. At first sight, it is true, one is surprised that the Pauline Epistles are not richer in allusions to the sayings of Christ, in view of their often vivid style, so suited to a pedagogical account. From this observation it has sometimes been concluded that Paul had not been instructed in the details of the life and preaching of Jesus and that, as a basis for his missionary activity and as a starting point for the whole of his theological system, he possessed only a condensed kerygma of a few lines, summarizing faith in the death and resurrection of Christ.[4] It is impossible here to go into the discussion of an opinion of this kind, and we must be satisfied with underlining the opinion of the majority of those who have studied the life of Paul. They have thought that it is more likely that after his conversion

[4]See, e.g., Bultmann, *Theology of the New Testament* (1952), pp. 187 f.

the apostle was instructed in what was an essential element of the spiritual treasure of the newborn church both in Palestine and in the Hellenistic world: the tradition touching what the savior had said and done during his life on earth. This is a presupposition of our work, the validity of which cannot be verified here, but which we must mention in view of the argument which follows.[5] We are, however, convinced that an analysis of certain themes of the parabolic language in the Pauline Epistles can support this conclusion, elaborated with the help of observations of quite another type: the apostle knew at least a part of the words of Christ, and he presupposed the same knowledge in the churches to which he addressed his letters.

Let us begin with a well-known passage where the allusion made by Paul to a saying of Christ is so clear that one can in principle give a positive reply to the question whether the apostle has referred to what he must have known from the teaching of Jesus. In characterizing the true Christian faith which ought to be dominated by love, Paul declares that it is insufficient to have "all faith, so as to remove mountains" if one does not have love (1 Cor. 13:2).[6] These words of Jesus are encountered three times in the synoptic Gospels, twice in Matthew (Matt. 17:20; 21:21; Mark 11:23), which shows the importance attributed to them in the early church. The coincidence between the Epistle and the Gospels, both as to the metaphor and the thought, is too striking to be mere chance. In spite of this reference of the apostle to a logion of Jesus, it may be shown, however, that it is not a question of a verbal quotation, but of an allusion which, being free in expression, relates to the essence of the metaphor in such a way that the recipients of the letter must have understood that the reminder of the

[5]See chap. 1, above; also published in *Studia Evangelica* (1959).
[6]Cf. James 1:6.

saying of Jesus was deliberate. For even those who had only heard this paradoxical saying of Christ once must without doubt have combined it immediately with the words of the apostle about faith removing mountains.

A whole group of metaphorical subjects are connected with organic life; the ideas of sowing and planting, growing and harvest. It could be said that these subjects are to be met with in the symbolism common to different religions, or at least that they are found many times in the Old Testament, which would suffice to explain the Pauline usage: the apostle was not a stranger to the religious language of the Hellenistic milieu and, furthermore, he knew even better the Holy Scripture of his people. It is also necessary to take into consideration, as Cerfaux has stressed,[7] the fact that these pictures of growth remained living in the Jewish apocalypses and also recurred in the Christian writings posterior to the New Testament, e.g., the Shepherd of Hermas. But let us stop a moment at the pictures of the sowing and harvest. They are met with several times in the Old Testament. The translation of the Septuagint offers the verbs σπείρω and θερίζω. Let us look closely at two passages chosen from the texts in question: "May those who sow in tears reap with shouts of joy! He that goes forth weeping, bearing the seed for sowing, shall come home with shouts of joy, bringing his sheaves with him" (Ps. 126:5 f. = 125:5 f. LXX).[8] "Do not sow in the furrows of injustice, for fear of harvesting sevenfold" (Sir. 7:3). The images present themselves here as pure analogies, to illustrate the natural or paradoxical relation between periods or actions in human life. However, a passage such as 1 Corinthians 9:11—"If

[7]L. Cerfaux, *The Church in the Theology of St. Paul* (New York: Herder Book Center, 1959); (cf. p. 10, n. 5).
[8]Cf. Jer. 12:13.

we have sown spiritual good among you, is it too much if we reap your material benefits?"—leaves quite a different impression. In this sentence, or at any rate in the first part of it, the allegorical language is not formed by spontaneous pictures, but presupposes a current usage of these metaphors in the terminology common to the writer and those he is addressing. An expression such as τὰ πνευματικὰ ἐσπείραμεν would have been impossible to understand without a previous knowledge of the spiritualized or allegorical idea of σπείρω. The part of the sentence, bearing on the harvest of material benefits which return to the apostle, has evidently been formed ad hoc, while sharing the allegorical sense of the first part. The case is the same in 2 Corinthians 9:6–10: "He who sows sparingly will also reap sparingly, and he who sows bountifully will also reap bountifully. Each one must do as he has made up his mind (9:6 f.). . . . He who supplies seed to the sower and bread for food will supply and multiply your resources and increase the harvest of your righteousness" (9:10). This time Paul has had recourse to the original picture, to the pure parable of the sowing and of the harvest found in 9:6, and this while sharing a preconceived idea which appears in 9:10. There the dominant word is σπείρω, the use of which here shows again that there must have been a metaphorical element in the Christian teaching of the period. In examining these verses we notice in fact that the metaphorical language of 9:10 could not be formed on the basis of the proverb of 9:6, but that quite to the contrary this has been quoted by the apostle to introduce the conclusion of 9:10 with the help of a current metaphor.

To summarize the allegorical use of the picture σπείρω or θερίζω in the Pauline Epistles, let us say that the mission of the apostle and the Christian activity of a local church are designated by the term of sowing, and this in view of the results of these activities. Now this terminology associates itself clearly with the Gospel parables of sowing and growing in Matthew 13, Mark 4, Luke 8, and above all to the explanation of the parable of the sower (Mark 4:14–20 and parallels). It is more precisely in the Gospel of Luke that we come upon the following expressions: ἐξῆλθεν ὁ σπείρων τοῦ σπεῖραι τὸν σπόρον αὐτοῦ (Luke 8:5) and ὁ σπόρος ἐστὶν ὁ λόγος τοῦ θεοῦ (8:11). One also finds in Mark the verbs αὐξάνω (Mark 4:8) and καρποφορέω (Mark 4:20 and parallels, cf. 2 Cor. 9:10).[9] In terms of these Gospel parables one can explain the likelihood of allegorical language around the metaphor of the sowing and the harvest in the catechism of the early church. We do not enter here into the discussion of the authenticity of the explanations of the parables of the sower and of the tares which may be read in the Gospels, but we are convinced that the allegorical usage to which our Gospels witness is earlier than the parabolic language of Paul and that it forms the basis for it.

Under these conditions the expression τὰ πνευματικὰ ἐσπείραμεν in the passage already quoted (1 Cor. 9:11) is worthy of a certain interest. As C. F. D. Moule has shown,[10] the adjective πνευματικός is to be found in the Christian catechism at first exactly as a complement to the metaphors indicating the new Christian realities: this is the case for example in οἶκος πνευματικός (1 Pet. 2:5) where the allegorization is intentional. Now the spiritual sowing comes back in Galatians 6:8 in a slightly more elaborate form: "For he who sows to his own flesh will from the flesh reap corruption [ὅτι ὁ σπείρων εἰς τὴν σάρκα ἑαυτοῦ ἐκ τῆς σαρκὸς θερίσει φθοράν]; but he who sows to the Spirit will from the Spirit reap eternal life [ὁ δὲ σπείρων εἰς τὸ πνεῦμα ἐκ τοῦ πνεύματος θερίσει ζωὴν αἰώνιον]. And let us not grow weary in well-doing [τὸ δὲ καλὸν ποιοῦντες μὴ ἐγκακῶμεν],

[9]See also Acts 6:7; 12:24.
[10]Moule, "Sanctuary and Sacrifice," pp. 29–41.

for in due season we shall reap, if we do not lose heart." Again the expression καιρῷ γὰρ ἰδίῳ θερίσομεν recalls the explanation of the parable of the sower (Mark 4:14–20 and parallels). The confrontation of the two harvests, corruption and eternal life, has a striking analogy in 1 Peter 1:23, where two kinds of sowing are characterized by the adjectives φθαρτός and ἄφθαρτος[11] which, once again, indicates the existence in the catechism of an allegorizing vocabulary about sowing and the harvest. This last passage from 1 Peter, followed by a quotation from Isaiah 40:6 f., also recalls the explanation of the parable of the sower. What is common to the allegorical metaphors in the texts which we have just mentioned is that they characterize the position of the disciple or of the Christian in the world, and that they stress the necessity of a life dominated by the Spirit.

The same picture or the same metaphorical theme comes back again in 1 Corinthians 15:36–44, the famous passage on the resurrection of the human body. But this time the picture develops another aspect of symbolism. The central point is here the fact that it is necessary for the grain of wheat to die in order to attain a new life. This is exactly the manner in which the subject has been developed in John 12:24: ἐὰν μὴ ὁ κόκκος τοῦ σίτου πεσὼν εἰς τὴν γῆν ἀποθάνῃ, αὐτὸς μόνος μένει. ἐὰν δὲ ἀποθάνῃ πολὺν καρπὸν φέρει. The difference is evidently that the Johannine passage is christological, while the Epistle to the Corinthians deals with the resurrection of the dead, but precisely on an analogy with the death and the resurrection of Christ. In another study we have tried to show that it is legitimate to claim a relationship between the symbolic theme of the parable of the sower and the christological application of the symbol of the grain

---

[11]Moule (pp. 33 f.) has underlined the affinity of λογικός and πνευματικός in contrast to σάρκινος.

193

of wheat in the Gospel of John.[12] In our opinion the reasoning of Paul in 1 Corinthians 15:36 ff. is an adaptation to the anthropology of the christological image preserved in the Fourth Gospel, which is to say that Paul knew this element which we no longer find except in the Johannine tradition. It is moreover in the line of the Pauline theology to present the big subjects of Christian anthropology by transposing the christological themes (cf. Rom. 6). The conformity of the expressions in John 12:24 and 1 Corinthians 15:36 f.— the grain of wheat (ὁ κόκκος τοῦ σίτου) being the central point of the symbolism and the clause ἐὰν μὴ . . . ἀποθάνῃ dominating the argument—is so evident, that it cannot be a fortuitous coincidence. In the continuation of the passage, we see that Paul has made use of a play on words in keeping with the terminology which we have thought we have been able to discern. Contrary to what is said in 1 Peter 1:23 of the perishable seed (σπόρος φθαρτός; cf. Gal. 6:8) Paul speaks, in a play on words, of the necessity of sowing in corruption (σπείρεται ἐν φθορᾷ) or rather of accepting destruction with a view to resurrection in incorruption (ἐγείρεται ἐν ἀφθαρσίᾳ, 1 Cor. 15:42).

If we cast a glance at the association of the complementary terms σπείρειν and θερίζειν in Galatians 6:7 f., we see that the apostle starts out from what is evidently a proverb: "Whatever a man sows, that he will also reap" (6:7). But the reasoning which follows is not carried out in accordance with the purely parabolic manner which characterized the use of these two complementary terms in the Old Testament.[13] As was the case in 1 Corinthians 9:11, we may once again establish that the argument which follows (Gal. 6:8) cannot be derived from the proverb, but that its object is to make the Galatians understand that it is necessary to

[12]See chap. 8, above.
[13]See especially Ps. 126:5 f.; Prov. 22:8; Sir. 7:3; Jer. 12:13; Hos. 10:12.

choose between two attitudes, two ways of life,[14] about which one knew in advance that they may be described by means of the allegory of the sowing and of the harvest.[15] The time of harvest is the moment when the seed produces its yield or simply gives its fruit. From that comes the use of the words ἐδίδου καρπόν and ἔφερεν in the parable of the sower and—what is more important for our study of the Pauline language—in its explanation (Mark 4:3–8, 14–20, and parallel). Let us recall Romans 15:27 f.: "If the Gentiles have come to share in their spiritual blessings [πνευματικοῖς], they ought also to be of service to them in material blessings [σαρκικοῖς, cf. 1 Cor. 9:11]. When therefore I have completed this, and have delivered to them what has been raised [τὸν καρπὸν τοῦτον], I shall go on by way of you to Spain" (cf. RSV, footnote). One may wonder if these words have not been formed with the help of the theme of the harvest, a solution which compels recognition if the word σφραγίζω, "to seal," here refers to the picture of the sacks of corn which have been sealed with a view to sale.[16]

The theme of the fruit, however, also appears in another figure or metaphor, evidently connected with that of the field of corn and in like manner known to the Old Testament and the Jewish tradition. It is the picture of the fruit tree which is a good bearer.[17] When Paul uses this theme, it is possible to show again that he does it in referring to a fixed allegory, which without doubt comes from the Gospel parables. The clearest case is perhaps Philippians 4:17 f.: "Not that I seek the gift; but I seek the fruit which increases to your credit [ἐπιζητῶ τὸν καρπὸν τὸν πλεονάζοντα εἰς λογόν

---

[14]Cf. Rom. 8:6, 13.
[15]Cf. John 4:36, a passage which is in harmony with 12:24, and also with Matt. 9:37 and its parallel, 13:30.
[16]See Bauer, *Greek-English Lexicon;* see further σφράγις.
[17]Concerning the symbolism of the tree (of life) see the article *Baum,* in *Reallexikon für Antike und Christentum,* vol. 1.

ὑμῶν]. I have received full payment, and more." We should like to see here an allusion to the parable of the barren fig tree of Luke 13:6–9 where the expression ζητῶν καρπόν occurs twice. It is, then, Paul in his capacity of apostle who comes to seek among the Philippians the fruits of their Christian life, and who received the gifts sent him by the church of the Philippians as a sign of the abundance of this life. We may wonder if a similar kind of idea lies behind these words from the exordium of the Epistle to the Romans (1:13): "in order that I may reap some harvest [ἵνα τινὰ καρπὸν σχῶ] among you as well as among the rest of the Gentiles." If such is the case, it is very characteristic that Paul—as he does elsewhere—here applies to his mission as apostle, seen in relation to the life of the church, messianic or christological pictures drawn from the Gospels.

The adjective ἄκαρπος, it is true, is sometimes met with in a sense so common or abstract that it is not worth the trouble of seeking in it a clearly defined picture.[18] But there is a text where the associations of the metaphor (or its background) perhaps become more visible. This is in a passage from the Pastoral Epistles, where in all probability the good deeds are characterized as good fruits, which gives to the sentence in question its full meaning: "And let our people learn to apply themselves to good deeds [καλῶν ἔργων] . . . and not be unfruitful [μὴ ὦσιν ἄκαρποι]" (Titus 3:14). Let us recall the words of John the Baptist and of Jesus about the tree which does not bear good fruit (μὴ ποιοῦν καρπὸν καλόν; Matt. 3:10 and parallel; cf. Luke 13:7).[19] And is it not the presence of the words of Jesus in the tradition which explain the question of Paul in Romans 6:21 (What fruit—or rather what sort of fruit—did you then gather?), where the continuation of the

---

[18] 1 Cor. 14:14; Eph. 5:11; ἄκαρπος is used in relation to the sowing in Matt. 13:22; Mark 4:19.
[19] Cr. ἀγαθος καρπάς in Matt. 7:17 ff.; 12:33; Luke 6:43.

text recalls a fruit which consists of sanctification and ends in eternal life? For the apostle without doubt knew the logion of Jesus about the good tree which gives good fruit and the bad tree which yields bad fruit (Matt. 7:16 ff.; 12:33; Luke 6:43 f.), and in addition he must have perceived that the Roman community knew not only the logion, but also its explanation in the parenesis. It is still within this range of ideas that the Pauline antithesis "bear fruit for God . . . bear fruit for death" (Rom. 7:4 f.) belongs. In Galatians 5:22 ff., a similarly parenetic passage, we learn what is "the fruit of the Spirit," while in opposition to this we have the "works [τὰ ἔργα] of the flesh" (5:19).[20] As to Colossians 1:10 ("bearing fruit in every good work and increasing in the knowledge of God"; cf. 1:6) it may even be suggested that the expression does not come from the picture of the field of wheat (in spite of the presence of the verb καρποφορέω in the parables of growing, e.g., Matt. 13:23; Mark 4:20, 28), but precisely from the figure of the fruit tree. We withhold this suggestion, however, for two reasons: on the one hand because of the complement καὶ αὐξανόμενοι τῇ ἐπιγνώσει τοῦ θεοῦ (1:10), and on the other hand because of the nature of the verbs καρποφορέω and αὐξάνω which are suitable for a tree yielding fruit and growing continuously; the nature would have been the opposite for a field of wheat. We also notice on examining the Pauline use of these metaphors that the eschatological point of the Gospel parables, where it is only a question of a final harvest or gathering in—the coming of the kingdom of God—has been toned down and adapted to a parenesis which rather had in view the continuous life of the church in the apostolic age.

In connection with the parabolic language about missionary work in 1 Corinthians 3:6–9, the commentators have

[20]Cf. Eph. 5:9, 11: καρπὸς τοῦ φωτός . . . τοῖς ἔργοις τοῖς ἀκάρποις τοῦ σκότους; Phil. 1:11: καρπὸν δικαιοσύνης. For Phil. 1:22, see for example the commentary of P. Bonnard (1950).

discussed the question whether the γεώργιον where Paul had planted and Apollos had watered is a field of wheat or a vineyard;[21] in this latter case it is necessary to remember that the vineyards of Palestine at the same time included other kinds of fruit trees. Already, if one examines the use of the word γεώργιον in the LXX, one is led to suppose that it is a question of an orchard.[22] Further, it appears that the verb γεωργέω is also habitually used there to indicate the plantation of vines. The word φυτεία, which is rare in the New Testament, is met with in an analogous sense[23] in the great allegory of the eagle in Ezekiel 17:1–8, an allegory with which the Pauline symbolism perhaps has an intentional affinity. For in the allegory of Ezekiel one of the two eagles plants the vine, while the other waters it to make shoots grow, to produce fruit (φέρειν καρπόν), and to make it into a noble vine (17:8). But contrary to the vine of Ezekiel, which is exposed to the judgment, the plantation about which Paul speaks will continue to exist, and this because Paul and Apollos have only been servants, each in the part assigned to him by God (1 Cor. 3:5).

On this subject it will be recalled, moreover, that the word φυτεία, which we had found in Ezekiel 17:7, occurs in Matthew 15:13: "Every plant which my heavenly Father has not planted will be rooted up." Does not this parabolic logion also allude to the allegory of Ezekiel, where the vine will be pulled from its roots (17:9)? Further, the Greek version of this prophetic saying presents the rare word σαπήσεται, "to rot," to indicate what will happen to the roots and the fruit of the vine (οὐχὶ αἱ ῥίζαι τῆς ἁπαλότητος αὐτῆς καὶ ὁ καρπὸς σαπήσεται; 17:9). It is possible that one must recognize in it one of the backgrounds to the whole of the

---

[21]Straub, Die Bildersprache, pp. 72 f.: "Ackerbau, nicht Gärtnerei."
[22]Prov., six times; Sir. 27. 6.
[23]Cf. 2 Kings 19:29; Mic. 1:6; Ps. Sol. 14:3–5.

logia of Jesus on fruit, where the rotten tree (τὸ σαπρὸν δένδρον) yields bad fruit (καρπὸς πονηρός).[24]

It is not by chance that the metaphors of planting and of growing are placed side by side with those of the building of a house in 1 Corinthians 3:6–17. The pictures there have a deep affinity as to the theological range of their symbolism, as is shown by a comparison with the parable of the sower (Mark 4:1–8) and with that of the houses built on rock and sand (Matt. 7:24–27 and parallel). Already in the Old Testament these two images have been placed side by side.[25]

However, let us look a little closer at the figure of the building of a house. In the words of Jesus it occurs with several variations: in the parable already mentioned (Matt. 7:24–27 and parallel), which concludes the Sermon on the Mount, in the quotation from Psalm 118:22 f. about the stone rejected by the builders (Mark 12:10 f. and parallel), and finally in the words addressed to Peter in Matthew 16:18. Although the three passages are, so to speak, christological, it is possible to show that the first is directed especially to the nature of the kingdom of God, the second to the mission of Christ, and the third to that of the disciple.

In the Pauline application it is in the first place the christological aspect of the figure which is taken up again. Christ is the foundation (θεμέλιον; 1 Cor. 3:11), as was the case of the rock in the Gospel parable (cf. Rom. 15:20). But, as in the Pauline metaphors of the sowing and harvest, it is also the mission of the disciple, that is, of both the apostle and of the Christian, which comes into view: "built upon the foundation of the apostles and prophets, Christ Jesus himself being the chief cornerstone [ἀκρογωνιαῖος]"[26] (Eph. 2:20; cf. Rev. 21:14). But where does the picture

[24]Cf. the use of the word ἄμπελος in Ezek. 17 and in John 15:1–6.
[25]E.g., Jer. 1:10; Sir. 49:7.
[26]See *Reallexikon für Antike und Christentum*, vol. 1: *Akrogoniaios*. It seems here to be a question of a foundation stone and not of a keystone.

come from of the Christians who form a building and who are identified with the construction (ἐποικοδομέω) of a holy temple? Is that a conception peculiar to Paul? No, not entirely. For there, too, it is possible to show a point of departure or background in a saying of Jesus which seems to have played an important part in the catechism of the early church. By way of argument we refer to the remark-able—and rather too little noticed—booklet of A. Cole.[27] The author demonstrates in a convincing way, in our opinion, that two Gospel passages (John 2:19, 21: "Destroy this temple, and in three days I will raise it up. . . . But he spoke of the temple of his body," and Matt. 26:61: the false witness before the Sanhedrin) reveal an authentic logion of Jesus about his body as a new temple. If this is the case, one may see there the point of departure of the Pauline conceptions of the body of Christ, as of the building of a holy temple in the savior. This does not prevent the theological development of the symbolism from being the work of the spirit of the apostle.[28] The coherence in the Pauline Epistles of the figures of the body, of the temple, and of the building (e.g., 1 Cor. 14; Eph. 2, 4) is best ex-plained by assuming the presence of a logion of the type we have just suggested in the words of Jesus transmitted by the tradition.

Among the pictures relating to the house and domestic life, following the example of the Gospels, we find in the Pauline Epistles the faithful servant (1 Cor. 4:1 f.; cf. Luke 12:42) and the heir (in connection with Christ and Chris-tians: Rom. 8:17; Col. 1:12; Mark 12:7 and parallel; Matt. 5:5; Mark 10:17 and parallel).[29]

[27]Cole, *The New Temple.*
[28]See further P. Vielhauer, *Oikodomè* (1941); O. Michel, οἰκοδομέω ναός, in Kittel, vol. 5 and vol. 4; *Reallexicon für Antike und Christentum,* vol. 1: *Bauen;* L. Cerfaux, *La Theologie de l'église,* pp. 185 f.
[29]We do not here go into the idea of κληρονόμος which seems to reveal the affinities between the teaching of Jesus and the thought of Paul.

The tripartite application of the metaphorical themes mentioned above, which in our opinion go back in the final analysis to the teaching of Jesus, is met in the symbolism of light as it appears in the Gospels. The kingdom of God is likened to a lamp which is put on a stand (Mark 4:21 f. and parallel; cf. Matt. 4:16). The disciples are the light of the world (Matt. 5:14, 16); at the same time they have the light within them (Matt. 6:22 f. and parallel; 13:43). But all this depends on Christ who is the light, a theme developed in the Fourth Gospel (John 8:12; cf. 1:4–9; 3:19–21; 12:35 f.). According to Paul, the new life is characterized by the light (Eph. 5:13; Col. 1:12; cf. 2 Cor. 4:6; 6:14). However, this has its source in Christ, who is the light (Eph. 5:14; 2 Tim. 1:10), and who at the time of his parousia will lighten the darkness (1 Cor. 4:5). Finally the Christians are not only in the light, but they also *are* light.[30] Thus Phil. 2:15 ("You shine as φωστῆρες in the world"; cf. Eph. 5:8) is probably a paraphrase of Matthew 5:16; the children of the light of 1 Thessalonians 5:5 recall Luke 16:8 (cf. John 12:35), and the "enlightened eyes" of Ephesians 1:18 have the appearance of being an adaptation of the Christian knowledge of Matthew 6:22 (cf. Luke 11:34–36) made by Paul with a view to his teaching. The expression ὁ γὰρ καρπὸς τοῦ φωτὸς ἐν πάσῃ αγαθωσύνη of Ephesians 5:9 ff. may reflect the juxtaposition of the light and the good works already found in Matthew 5:16.

The theme of vigilance, already examined by Selwyn[31] as one of the elements of the parenesis of apostolic times, is recalled with a very clear eschatological accent by Paul in 1 Thessalonians 5:6: "So then let us not sleep, as others do, but let us keep awake [γρηγορῶμεν] and be sober."[32]

---

[30]For this conception, see H. Schlier, *Der Brief an die Epheser* (1957), pp. 236 f.
[31]Selwyn, *First Epistle of St. Peter*, pp. 377 f., 447.
[32]Cf. 1 Cor. 16:13.

The figure comes again in Ephesians 6:18 (ἀγρυπνέω) linked to the exhortation to prayer.[33] This clearly resembles Luke 12:35–38, a passage which contains a whole compendium of vigilance. But the matter is not quite so simple. It should be asked whether the text of Luke has not been written precisely on the basis of the catechism of the church, in such a way that even the Pauline Epistles have been able to influence it. But the passage in Luke may indicate to us where the subject comes from, and that it seems to have two sources in the words of Jesus: the parable of the ten virgins (Matt. 25:1–13), where the conclusion "Watch therefore [γρηγορεῖτε], for you know neither the day nor the hour" (25:13) has without doubt been added very early,[34] and the parable of the servants waiting for the master of the house (Mark 13:34–36 and parallel), a parable which has also formed part of the eschatological teaching of Jesus.[35]

The parable of the ten virgins, moreover, contains a figure the symbolic usage of which seems to have been taken up again by Paul. It is the picture of the wedding, closely connected with that of the bridegroom (νυμφίος; Matt. 25:1, 10; Mark 2:19 and parallel).[36] In our opinion it is probable that Jesus used this picture to indicate in a symbolic way his own person, thus alluding to the passages in the Old Testament which describe Yahweh as the bridegroom of Israel.[37] In developing this theme Paul speaks of the church, seen in its relation to Christ, as an espoused virgin or bride, now referring to a local community (2 Cor.

---

[33]For the connection between vigilance and prayer, see Matt. 26:41 and Mark 14:38, which differ from Luke 22:39–46.

[34]Cf. Rom. 13:11.

[35]For the theme of the Day of the Lord which comes like a thief in the middle of the night: 1 Thess. 5:2, 4; cf. Matt. 24:42–44; Luke 12:39 f.

[36]Cf. J. Jeremias, νύμφη, νυμφίος, Kittel, vol. 4; E. Stauffer, γαμέω, γάμος, in Kittel, vol. 1.

[37]E.g., Isa. 50:1; 54:6–7; Ezek. 16 and 23; Hos. 2; Song of Solomon; cf. Rev. 21:2.

11:2), now inserting into a parenetic passage a whole elaborated ecclesiology (Eph. 5:25–32).[38]

The theme of the struggle against the diabolical powers with its numerous pictures is too complicated to be approached in a preliminary and restricted study as this. Let us briefly indicate that it may be asked if the way in which Paul treats this subject[39] has points of contact with the Gospel parable about the armed man who is overcome in his own palace, and above all with the form this parable has in Luke (11:21 f.; cf. Matt. 12:29; Mark 3:27).

The few points of view presented here have been grouped in a simple outline and only give impressions gathered during the course of reading the Epistles of Paul. If Paul has really taken up the parabolic themes transmitted by tradition, a tradition he must have known, the fact in no way prejudices the creative achievement of the apostle when he created the incomparable themes of his letters. On the contrary it may be said that the literary and theological genius of Paul appears precisely in the manner in which he takes up, develops, and applies these metaphorical themes while preserving the actual substance of their original meaning. Moreover, in the Pauline Epistles there is a fund of other pictures and metaphors which should certainly also be taken into account in the study of the style of the Epistles as a whole, in measuring especially the intellectual effort which Paul must have made in order to render the Christian message understandable to those whom he addressed.

If one may say that the Pauline Christology is in a certain sense a development of the teaching of Jesus about the mission of the Son of man—but a development which is

[38]Cerfaux, *La theologie de l'église*, pp. 262 ff.; Ernest Best, *One Body in Christ* (New York: Macmillan, 1955), pp. 169–83; Schlier, *Der Brief*; cf. Gal. 4:21–31.
[39]Esp. in Eph. 6:10–17; cf. 2 Cor. 6:7; 10:4.

creative in the highest degree—the presence in the Epistles of parabolic pictures borrowed from the sayings of Jesus can teach us that Paul has remained in continual contact with the tradition concerning the words and deeds of Jesus, a tradition which has resulted in our Gospels. Such an indication may be illuminating for all studies of Pauline theology.

However, because of the discreet way in which Paul used the parabolic themes which he borrowed from the Gospel tradition—a discretion which we consider to be intentional—it is scarcely possible to determine in which phase of its development this tradition was when Paul made use of it, nor to determine whether it was an oral tradition—which is, however, the most probable—or already written, whether it was the tradition called "synoptic" or even a certain current within this. Apart from these questions, a thorough examination of the parabolic language in the Pauline Epistles would, however, likely succeed in casting some light on the evolution of the thought of the apostle and on the way in which he formed his Gospel and his parenesis.

Indexes

I. Index of Source Citations

1. OLD TESTAMENT

2. APOCRYPHAL AND OTHER LATE JEWISH LITERATURE

3. NEW TESTAMENT

Indexes

Indexes

211

4. ANCIENT AND EARLY CHURCH WRITERS

Indexes

ORIGEN
Contra Celsum 8. 22 – 124

PLINY THE YOUNGER
Epistle 96. 7 – 128

PEREGRINATIO AETHERIAE 24. 9 f.
– 129

TERTULLIAN
De Pudicitia 8 f. – 140
De Pudicitia 13 – 105

II. Index of Names